zest

acknowledgments

A heartfelt thanks to Kay Scarlett and Juliet Rogers for the chance to take an idea and turn it into a beautiful book, and to Jackie Frank for giving me the opportunity to do it. As well a huge thank you to Marylouise Brammer and Victoria Carey for their tireless work and enthusiasm in bringing this book to fruition. Indeed, a big thank you to the whole team at Murdoch Books for getting behind these projects and never lagging in their enthusiasm and trust.

In the studio, the "family" came together once again. A big hug to Ross Dobson who proved yet again to be the patron saint of beautiful food, good humour and great coffee. This book would not have been possible without all your hard work, seamless preparation and day-to-day assistance. Not to mention the running commentary on the state of the world and the daily crossword puzzle. To Margot Braddon, a big thank you for all your running around in search of colour and surface.

As always, this book would not have been possible without Petrina Tinslay. There isn't a thank you or a hug big enough to cover the debt of beautiful photographs, generosity and kindness, daily mothering, calm assurance, the day-to-day fun and good times and the hourly admonishments to not pick anything up! I certainly couldn't have done it without you so thank you, thank you, thank you for everything. Thank you also to Petrina's wonderful assistants, Laura and Petrina, for their constant attention to detail and unflagging good humour in the face of yet another piece of fabric to iron.

To the final member of the studio team, who at the time of writing still remains nameless — although he or she has been travelling under the pseudonym Norbert while in the studio! — thank you for not hurrying into the world and allowing me to finish this book. Thanks also to Mum and Dad for always being there and to Warwick for his constant support, tireless enthusiasm and the simple fact that I always walk into a house filled with love and laughter.

A book about food needs the best starting point. So thank you to Hugh and Justin at Murdoch Produce for their great fruit and vegetables and also Vic's Meats and Demcos Seafoods for their fantastic produce.

A huge thank you also has to go to David Edmonds for his generosity and sublimely beautiful ceramics and to Mud Australia for their delicate bowls. Thanks also to Orson & Blake and The Bay Tree for their beautiful homewares.

Copublished in 2003 by special arrangement between Murdoch Books® and Graphic Arts Center Publishing®.

ISBN 1-55868-773-4

Distributed in the United States of America by Graphic Arts Center Publishing Company
P.O. Box 10306, Portland, OR 97296-0306
Telephone (503) 226-2402; Web site www.gacpc.com

Published by Murdoch Books®, a division of Murdoch Magazines Pty Ltd.

Author and Stylist: Michele Cranston
Photographer: Petrina Tinslay
Creative Director: Marylouise Brammer
Food Preparation: Ross Dobson
Editorial Project Manager: Victoria Carey
Production: Fiona Byrne

Chief Executive: Juliet Rogers
Publisher: Kay Scarlett

Printed by Toppan Printing Hong Kong Co. Ltd. PRINTED IN CHINA. First printed 2003.

The publisher would like to thank the following for their assistance with photography:
AEG Kitchen Appliances, Liebherr Refrigeration and Wine Cellars; Breville Holdings Pty Ltd.

Those at risk from the effects of salmonella food poisoning (including the elderly, pregnant women and children) should consult their GP with any concerns about eating raw eggs.

zest

michele cranston

photography by
petrina tinslay

Graphic Arts Center Publishing®

contents

A beautiful twist of lemon peel or a thirst for new and exciting flavours? Zest can mean many things, but when I thought of the title for this book, I wanted to capture the essence of our ever-changing global cuisine. A zest for wonderful flavours and foods, an enthusiasm for crossing culinary boundaries and a desire to savour all things new. From the verdant green basil leaves of Italy to the ruby-red chillies of Mexico, *Zest* is inspired by world food. Who can choose between the Mediterranean's silvery sage leaves and fragrant rosemary, or the intoxicating spices from the Middle East or the tangy twist of South-East Asia? Tall elegant

a zest for flavour

stalks of fresh lemon grass, glossy limes and chillies in all shapes and sizes are now piled high on the market tables of the world. The intoxicating scent of cinnamon quills lures you into spice shops with shelves laden with culinary treasure. Discover the magic that tiny golden strands of saffron can bring to the table or experience the aromatic delight of ground cumin. Once exotic, these foods are becoming increasingly familiar as we explore new things. It's all about a zest for flavour.

savour

Rosemary, basil, sage, parsley, mint and thyme — the herbs of Mediterranean climes. Imagine a lunch in the sun without them. Robust in style, simple dishes are transformed by their addition. From the emerald-green sprigs of garden-fresh parsley to the elegant silver-grey leaves of sage, some would say they have had the greatest influence of all on global cuisine. Enjoy the peppery thyme, in all its guises, and the lushness of basil leaves in salads or tossed over seared tuna. Aromatic rosemary, with its woody stems and spiky leaves, infuses everything from wintry broths to richly baked lamb with the most delicious flavour while sage, that most handsome of herbs, makes the perfect companion to Parmesan veal and other savoury dishes. Bring a freshness to the table with mint or transform a meal with generous amounts of parsley. Fresh and simple, these are the herbs to savour.

marinated bocconcini salad

octopus salad

6–8 small desiree potatoes
2 lemons, juiced
4 garlic cloves
10–12 sprigs thyme
8 small baby octopus, cleaned
2 handfuls baby rocket (arugula) leaves
2 handfuls flat-leaf (Italian) parsley leaves
60 g (1/3 cup) small black olives
3 tablespoons extra virgin olive oil
1 lemon, cut into wedges

Put the potatoes in a large pot and fill with cold water. Add 1 tablespoon of sea salt, lemon juice, garlic and thyme. Bring to the boil and cook for 10 minutes. Add the octopus and continue to cook for another 10 minutes. Remove from the heat and allow the octopus and potatoes to cool in the water. When cool, remove the potatoes and octopus and cut them into bite-sized chunks. Divide the rocket and most of the parsley between four plates. Arrange the potatoes and octopus over the leaves. Scatter with the olives and garnish with the remaining parsley. Lightly season with sea salt and freshly ground black pepper then drizzle with the olive oil. Serve with lemon wedges. Serves 4 as a starter

marinated bocconcini salad

3 tablespoons extra virgin olive oil
1 handful flat-leaf (Italian) parsley leaves
1 tablespoon thyme leaves
10 mint leaves, roughly torn
2 tablespoons finely chopped chives
10 basil leaves, roughly torn
4 bocconcini, cut into quarters
24 small black olives
2 tablespoons balsamic vinegar

Put the olive oil, parsley, thyme, mint, chives and basil in a bowl. Add the bocconcini and toss until it is well coated. Season with sea salt and cracked black pepper and set aside for 1 hour or overnight to marinate.

Pile the marinated cheese into a serving bowl and scatter with the olives. Finish with a drizzle of balsamic vinegar and season to taste. Serves 4 as a salad

beetroot dip

4 large beetroot
250 g (1 cup) Greek-style yoghurt
1 teaspoon pomegranate molasses
10 mint leaves, finely chopped
10 walnuts, finely chopped
toasted Lebanese bread

Preheat the oven to 200°C (400°F/Gas 6). Place the beetroot in a baking dish with 250 ml (1 cup) of water. Cover with foil and bake for 1 hour, or until cooked. Carefully rub the skin off the beetroot with your fingers—wearing rubber gloves to prevent your hands from getting stained.

Place the beetroot in a food processor or blender and blend into a smooth paste. Put into a bowl and stir in the yoghurt and molasses. Season to taste with sea salt and freshly ground black pepper. Garnish with the mint and walnuts and serve with toasted Lebanese bread. Serves 6–8 as a dip

fresh and fast

- Sear baby octopus quickly on a hot grill (broiler) and toss with fresh herb leaves, olive oil and lemon juice. Serve with olives and roughly chopped tomatoes.
- Finely chop all the ingredients of the bocconcini salad and pile onto lightly toasted and oiled sourdough bread for an easy bruschetta topping.
- Roughly chop several baked and peeled beetroots and toss with fresh mint and finely sliced red onion. Drizzle with olive oil and pomegranate molasses. Serve with seared lamb.
- Finely slice bocconcini and add to a salad of baby rocket (arugula) leaves, roughly chopped tomatoes, finely sliced spring onions (scallions) and pan-fried salami slices. Add the warm salami oil from the pan to the salad with a little balsamic vinegar.

beetroot dip

prosciutto and sugar snap salad

3 tablespoons olive oil
8 slices prosciutto
2 fennel bulbs, finely shaved
200 g (7 oz) sugar snap peas, blanched and sliced on the diagonal
10 mint leaves, torn
1 lemon, juiced

Heat the olive oil in a large frying pan over a medium heat and fry the prosciutto until lightly crisp. Set aside to drain on paper towels. Put the fennel, peas and mint into a bowl. Drizzle with the oil from the pan and the lemon juice. Break the crisp prosciutto into small pieces and add to the salad. Toss together and divide between four plates. Serves 4 as a starter

artichoke, parsley and caper spaghetti

1 x 340 g (12 oz) jar marinated artichoke hearts, drained and finely chopped
30 g (1/2 cup) roughly chopped flat-leaf (Italian) parsley
1 lemon, zest grated
2 tablespoons salted capers, rinsed well
3 handfuls baby English spinach leaves
50 g (1 3/4 oz) Parmesan cheese, grated
2 tablespoons extra virgin olive oil
400 g (14 oz) spaghetti

Bring a large pot of salted water to the boil. Put the artichoke hearts, parsley, lemon zest, lemon juice, capers, spinach, Parmesan and half the extra virgin olive oil into a large bowl and stir until combined.

Cook the spaghetti in the boiling water until *al dente*, then drain and add to the bowl. Stir until the spaghetti is well coated then drizzle with the remaining olive oil. Divide between four pasta bowls and serve immediately. Season with freshly ground black pepper. Serves 4

salad of sweet onions and prosciutto

2 tablespoons olive oil
8 slices prosciutto, cut in half
12 spring onions (scallions), trimmed and sliced in half
1 small bunch thyme
1 tablespoon brown sugar
2 tablespoons balsamic vinegar
125 ml (1/2 cup) red wine
2 ripe tomatoes, finely diced
1 radicchio (chicory), trimmed and leaves washed
4 slices rye bread, toasted
2 tablespoons extra virgin olive oil

Heat the olive oil in a large frying pan over a medium heat and fry the prosciutto until lightly crisp. Drain on paper towels. Add the spring onions to the pan with the thyme sprigs. Reduce the heat to low, sprinkle with the sugar and add the vinegar and wine. Cover and cook slowly for 10 minutes.

Place the tomato into a bowl and season with sea salt and freshly ground black pepper. Remove the lid from the spring onions and place the radicchio over the spring onions for a few minutes, or until it begins to wilt. Toss the spring onions and tomato together.

To assemble, place the rye toast on four plates. Top with the radicchio, spoon over the tomato and spring onions then top with the prosciutto. Drizzle with extra virgin olive oil and serve immediately. Serves 4 as a starter

fennel remoulade

2 egg yolks
1 lemon, juiced
250 ml (1 cup) oil
1 tablespoon Dijon mustard
3 large fennel bulbs, trimmed
1 handful flat-leaf (Italian) parsley leaves
4 slices heavy rye bread, toasted

Whisk the egg yolks and lemon juice together in a large bowl. Slowly drizzle in the oil, whisking constantly, until the mixture becomes thick and creamy. Stir in the mustard and season to taste with sea salt. Set the mayonnaise aside.

Slice the fennel into paper-thin slices then roughly chop. Add to the mayonnaise and stir until the fennel is well coated then add the parsley. Serve a large spoonful of the remoulade with rye toast. Serves 4 as a starter

fish, clam and herb soup

capsicum salad

fish, clam and herb soup

500 g (1 lb 2 oz) live clams or vongole in the shell
4 tablespoons olive oil
2 onions, finely chopped
2 garlic cloves, minced
1/2 teaspoon thyme leaves
1/2 teaspoon smoky paprika
14 sage leaves, 2 finely chopped
1/2 teaspoon finely chopped rosemary leaves
125 ml (1/2 cup) white wine
4 large ripe tomatoes, finely diced
2 large potatoes, finely diced
2 tablespoons tomato paste (purée)
500 g (1 lb 2 oz) white fish fillets, cut into bite-sized pieces
3 tablespoons finely chopped flat-leaf (Italian) parsley

Soak the clams in water for 10 minutes, discarding any that don't close when tapped. Heat half the oil in a saucepan over a medium heat. Add the onions, garlic, thyme, paprika, chopped sage and rosemary. Cook until the onions are transparent then add the wine and clams. Cover and cook for 1 minute. When the clams have opened, remove and set aside. Add the tomato, potato, paste and 750 ml (3 cups) of water. Simmer for 10 minutes then add the fish and cook for another 5 minutes. Meanwhile, fry the sage leaves in the remaining oil until crispy. Add the parsley and clams to the soup then garnish with crispy sage leaves. Serves 4

capsicum salad

2 red capsicums (peppers)
2 garlic cloves, finely sliced
4 anchovies, finely chopped
4 small ripe Roma (plum) tomatoes, halved
80 ml (1/3 cup) olive oil
1 handful flat-leaf (Italian) parsley leaves
2 witlof (chicory/Belgian endive), washed and finely sliced
2 boiled eggs, finely chopped
1 tablespoon salted capers, well rinsed

Preheat the oven to 200°C (400°F/Gas 6). Cut the capsicums in half and remove any seeds. Put the capsicum halves, open side up, on a baking tray. Scatter with the garlic and anchovies. Place a tomato half inside each capsicum half, drizzle with the olive oil and season with sea salt and freshly ground black pepper. Bake for 1 hour.

Divide the parsley and witlof between four plates. Put a capsicum half on each plate. Scatter with the chopped egg and capers. Drizzle with the pan juices and serve immediately. Serves 4

braised mushrooms with buttered angel hair pasta

700 g (1 lb 9 oz) mixed mushrooms (button, Swiss brown, shiitake, oyster and enoki)
3 tablespoons olive oil
3 garlic cloves, crushed
1 tablespoon fresh thyme leaves
250 ml (1 cup) white wine
250 g (9 oz) fresh angel hair pasta or dried linguine
2 tablespoons butter
2 tablespoons finely chopped flat-leaf (Italian) parsley
4 tablespoons finely grated Parmesan cheese

Bring a large pot of salted water to the boil. Cut the mushrooms into halves or quarters. Heat the oil in a large saucepan over a medium heat and add the garlic, mushrooms and thyme. Toss the mushrooms in the pan and cook until the garlic begins to soften. Add the white wine and season with sea salt. Cover with a lid and simmer for 7 minutes. Add the pasta to the water and cook until *al dente*. Drain the pasta then put it back in the hot saucepan. Stir the butter and parsley through the pasta then pile onto four warmed plates. Make a well in the centre of the pasta and fill with the mushrooms. Drizzle with the mushroom cooking liquid and season with freshly ground black pepper. Serve sprinkled with the Parmesan. Serves 4 as a starter

fresh and fast

- Make an easy pasta sauce using some of the flavours in the capsicum salad. Finely chop Roma (plum) tomatoes and toss them with anchovies, capers, parsley leaves and a generous drizzle of olive oil. Toss with your favourite pasta and serve with some freshly grated Parmesan cheese.
- Pan-fry a selection of mushrooms with a little crushed garlic, a sprig or two of fresh thyme, butter and a splash of white wine. Season and serve with grilled steak.
- Prepare the clams as per the recipe for the soup. Heat some oil into a large frying pan and sauté garlic, onions, a little rosemary and sage. Cook until the onions are transparent, then add some wine and the clams. Cover and cook for 1 minute. Add freshly cooked *al dente* pasta and a splash of cream. Serve with a scatter of finely grated Parmesan cheese and fresh parsley.
- Make a quick salad of finely sliced endive leaves, orange segments, fresh parsley leaves and small black olives.

braised mushrooms with buttered angel hair pasta

bean salad with cherry tomatoes and haloumi

Garden-fresh beans, unblemished and crisp, add a fresh bite to any salad.

sage and parmesan veal chops

bean salad with cherry tomatoes and haloumi

150 g (5$^{1}/_{2}$ oz) French beans, trimmed
200 g (7 oz) flat green beans, trimmed
1 tablespoon lemon juice
2 tablespoons extra virgin olive oil
250 g (1 punnet) cherry tomatoes, cut into quarters
1 handful mint leaves
1 handful basil leaves
250 g (9 oz) haloumi cheese (glossary)
1 tablespoon olive oil

Slice the French beans into halves and the flat beans into 1 cm ($^{1}/_{2}$ in) lengths. Set aside. Put the lemon juice and extra virgin olive oil into a large bowl and season with a little sea salt and freshly ground black pepper. Bring a pot of salted water to the boil. Add the beans and cook until the French beans are bright green. Quickly drain and toss the beans in the lemon juice and olive oil. When the beans are cool, add the cherry tomatoes, mint and basil leaves. Cut the haloumi into 8 slices. Heat the olive oil in a frying pan over a high heat and fry the haloumi pieces on both sides until golden brown. Put a haloumi slice on each serving plates. Spoon the bean salad over then top with the remaining pieces of haloumi. Serves 4 as a starter

sage and parmesan veal chops

4 sage leaves
80 g (1 cup) fresh breadcrumbs
4 tablespoons grated Parmesan cheese
2 tablespoons roughly chopped flat-leaf (Italian) parsley
2 eggs
4 x 200 g (7 oz) veal chops
2 tablespoons butter
2 tablespoons olive oil
lemon wedges
green salad

Preheat the oven to 200°C (400°F/Gas 6). Put the sage leaves, breadcrumbs, Parmesan and parsley into a food processor. Season with $^{1}/_{2}$ teaspoon of sea salt and some freshly ground black pepper, then process until fine breadcrumbs form. Beat the eggs in a bowl and set aside. Dip each cutlet into the egg mixture then press firmly into the breadcrumbs. Heat the butter and olive oil in a large frying pan over a medium to high heat. Cook the cutlets for 2 minutes on each side then bake for 12 minutes. Serve with lemon wedges and a green salad. Serves 4

tuna with roast capsicums

rice with vermicelli, parsley and puy lentils

seared tuna with capsicums and anchovies

2 tablespoons vegetable oil
2 red capsicums (peppers)
4 anchovies, roughly chopped
1 handful flat-leaf (Italian) parsley leaves
12 basil leaves
4 tablespoons extra virgin olive oil
4 x 150 g (5 1/2 oz) tuna steaks
2 handfuls baby English spinach leaves
1 tablespoon balsamic vinegar

Heat half the oil in a frying pan over a high heat. Add the capsicums and sear, turning occasionally, until they are blistered on all sides. Transfer to a bowl and cover with plastic wrap. When the capsicums are cool, remove the seeds, stalk and any skin that rubs off easily, making sure you catch the liquid in the bowl. Slice the capsicums into thin strips and put into another bowl. Strain the liquid from the original bowl over them. Add the anchovies, parsley, basil and extra virgin olive oil. Season with freshly ground black pepper. Heat the remaining oil in the frying pan over a high heat. Add the tuna steaks and sear them on one side for 1 minute. Turn the tuna over, reduce the heat to medium and cook for a further 3 to 4 minutes. Divide the spinach between four plates, top with tuna and spoon over the capsicum salad. Drizzle with a little balsamic vinegar and serve. Serves 4

goat's cheese salad with celery, pear and parsley

1 tablespoon white wine vinegar
3 tablespoons extra virgin olive oil
3 celery stalks, finely sliced
3 nashi pears, finely sliced
1 handful flat-leaf (Italian) parsley leaves
25 g (1/4 cup) flaked almonds, toasted
150 g (5 1/2 oz) goat's cheese

Put the vinegar and extra virgin olive oil into a large bowl. Season with sea salt and freshly ground black pepper. Stir to combine, then add the celery, pear, parsley and almonds. Toss, then pile onto a serving platter. Crumble the goat's cheese over the salad and serve immediately. Serves 4

rice with vermicelli, parsley and puy lentils

5 tablespoons olive oil
3 garlic cloves, crushed
3 red onions, finely sliced
2 teaspoons ground cumin
1 egg vermicelli nest
250 g (9 oz) basmati rice
100 g (3 1/2 oz) Puy lentils
1 handful flat-leaf (Italian) parsley leaves, roughly chopped
tahini sauce (basics)

Heat 2 tablespoons of the olive oil in a frying pan and add the garlic, onions and cumin. Cook over a medium heat, stirring occasionally until the onions are dark brown and caramelized. Meanwhile, heat the remaining 3 tablespoons of oil in a large saucepan over a medium heat. Crush the vermicelli nest in your hands and add to the oil. Stir until the noodles are golden then add the rice and lentils. Stir together before adding 800 ml (28 fl oz) of water and a heaped teaspoon of sea salt. Bring to the boil then reduce the heat to low, cover with a lid and simmer for 20 minutes, or until the water is absorbed. Stir in the caramelized onions and spoon into a serving bowl. Garnish with the parsley leaves and serve with the tahini sauce. Serve with roast chicken or spicy sausages. Serves 4 as a side dish

fresh and fast

- Make a fresh salad of pear and watercress and serve with finely sliced roast duck breast.
- Finely dice roast capsicums (peppers) and toss together with some finely sliced anchovies, basil leaves and black olives. Drizzle with olive oil and a dash of balsamic vinegar. Serve piled over grilled steak or lamb fillets.
- Heat 2 tablespoons of oil in a frying pan and add a little crushed garlic, 4 finely sliced red onions and 2 teaspoons of ground cumin. Cook over a low heat until the onions are caramelized. Add 125 ml (1/2 cup) of red wine and simmer for a few minutes before serving with grilled pork sausages.
- Make a quick and easy salad of finely sliced leg ham, Parmesan cheese, sliced pear and rocket (arugula) leaves. Serve with fingers of oiled and toasted sourdough bread.

goat's cheese salad with celery, pear and parsley

thyme and sumac-seared tuna with minted potatoes

Sumac, a peppery spice of the Middle East, is balanced by the sweet freshness of mint.

lamb cutlets with tomato and parsley salad

thyme and sumac-seared tuna with minted potatoes

600 g (1 lb 5 oz) kipfler or new potatoes
1 tablespoon finely chopped fresh thyme
3 tablespoons finely chopped chives
3 tablespoons sumac
1 x 500 g (1 lb 2 oz) tuna fillet, cut into smaller fillets
2 tablespoons olive oil
6 tablespoons extra virgin olive oil
1 tablespoon lemon juice
1 handful mint leaves

Put the potatoes in a large pot of cold water with 1 tablespoon of sea salt and bring to the boil over a high heat. When the water reaches boiling point, cover with a lid and remove from the heat. Leave the potatoes to sit for 30 minutes. Put the thyme, chives and sumac onto a plate and roll the tuna in the herbs until each fillet is well covered.

Heat a large frying pan over a high heat and add the olive oil. Sear the tuna fillets for 2 minutes on each side then remove the pan from the heat. Allow the tuna to sit in the pan until ready to serve.

To make the dressing, mix together 4 tablespoons of extra virgin olive oil and lemon juice in a small bowl. Drain the potatoes and return them to the warm pot. Using a large spoon, roughly break up the potatoes and add the remaining extra virgin olive oil. Season with sea salt and freshly ground black pepper.

Slice the tuna into bite-sized pieces and serve on top of the potatoes. Scatter with the mint leaves and drizzle with dressing. Serves 4

lamb cutlets with tomato and parsley salad

4 tablespoons couscous
1 teaspoon butter
2 teaspoons ground cumin
3 ripe Roma (plum) tomatoes, sliced into a thick dice
1 Lebanese (short) cucumber, sliced into a thick dice
1/2 red onion, finely diced
1 handful flat-leaf (Italian) parsley, roughly chopped
1 tablespoon balsamic vinegar
3 tablespoons extra virgin olive oil
8 lamb cutlets

Put the couscous in a bowl and add the butter, cumin and 125 ml (1/2 cup) of boiling water. Cover and allow to soak for 2 to 3 minutes.

Meanwhile, make the tomato and parsley salad, by combining the tomatoes, cucumber, onion, parsley, vinegar and olive oil in a large bowl. Season with sea salt and freshly ground black pepper and stir until all the ingredients are coated in the dressing. Fluff the couscous with a fork then toss it through the salad. Barbecue or grill (broil) the cutlets for 2 to 3 minutes on each side. Remove from the heat, season with sea salt and rest for 1 minute. Spoon the salad onto four serving plates and top with the cutlets. Serves 4

barley and bacon soup

lamb shank with white beans

barley and bacon soup

2 tablespoons butter
2 garlic cloves, minced
3 leeks, washed and finely chopped
1 teaspoon fresh thyme leaves
1/2 teaspoon finely chopped rosemary leaves
4 bacon rashers, finely diced
1 large carrot, grated
2 celery sticks, finely sliced
175 g (6 oz) pearl barley
2 litres (8 cups) chicken or vegetable stock
1 handful flat-leaf (Italian) parsley leaves
50 g (1 3/4 oz) grated Parmesan cheese

Melt the butter in a large saucepan over a medium heat and add the garlic and leeks. Stir for 1 minute before adding the thyme, rosemary and bacon. Continue to cook until the leeks are soft and transparent. Add the carrot, celery and barley and cook for a further 5 minutes, stirring. Pour in the stock, cover with a lid and reduce the heat to a simmer. Cook for 1 hour, or until the barley is soft.

Ladle the hot soup into four bowls and top with the parsley leaves and Parmesan. Serves 4

fennel and tomato salad

3 fennel bulbs, trimmed
1 tablespoon fresh thyme leaves
2 tablespoons lemon juice
8 tablespoons extra virgin olive oil
500 g (1 lb 2 oz) truss tomatoes, stalks intact
1 tablespoon balsamic vinegar
1 teaspoon caster (superfine) sugar
70 g (2 1/2 oz) Parmesan cheese, shaved
1 handful basil leaves

Preheat the oven to 200°C (400°F/Gas 6). Cut the fennel bulbs from top to base into several thick slices. Place on a baking tray with the thyme, drizzle with the lemon juice and 4 tablespoons of olive oil. Cover with foil and put in the oven.

Place the tomatoes on another smaller baking tray and drizzle with the vinegar and remaining olive oil. Sprinkle with the sugar, cover with foil and put in the oven. Bake the tomatoes and fennel for 30 minutes, or until the tomatoes are beginning to burst.

To assemble, layer the fennel, tomatoes and shaved Parmesan with the basil leaves. Spoon over the cooking liquids and serve with warm crusty bread. Serves 4 as a starter

lamb shank with white beans

125 g (1 cup) plain (all-purpose) flour
4 lamb shanks (about 1.2 kg/2 lb 12 oz)
8 tablespoons olive oil
1 large red onion, finely sliced
2 garlic cloves, crushed
1 teaspoon rosemary leaves
1 celery stick, diced
2 carrots, thinly sliced into rounds
200 g (1 cup) dried haricot beans, soaked overnight
500 ml (2 cups) veal stock (basics)
125 ml (1/2 cup) dry Marsala
horseradish gremolata (basics)

Preheat the oven to 200°C (400°F/Gas 6). Put the flour in a plastic bag, add the shanks and toss until well coated. Heat half the olive oil in a casserole dish. Add the shanks and turn until they are browned on all sides. Remove from the heat and set aside. Heat the remaining oil in a frying pan over a medium heat. Add the onion, garlic and rosemary and cook until the onion is soft and lightly golden. Spoon the onion, celery, carrot and soaked beans over the lamb shanks then add the stock and Marsala. Cover and bake in the oven for 2 hours, moving the shanks around in the liquid halfway through. Remove from the oven and serve with a sprinkle of the horseradish gremolata. Serves 4

fresh and fast

- Finely slice a fennel bulb and toss with extra virgin olive oil, lemon zest, lemon juice and finely chopped flat-leaf (Italian) parsley. Toss together and season with sea salt and white pepper. Allow to sit for 30 minutes then serve with grilled tuna and a salad of boiled new potatoes.
- Bake 4 small vines of truss tomatoes with a little oil and balsamic vinegar until the tomatoes are beginning to split. Serve with grilled steak and garnish with a scatter of grated fresh horseradish and a drizzle of pan juices.
- Slow-bake several lamb shanks with red wine, garlic and roughly chopped onions and tomatoes. Remove the meat from the shanks and roughly chop. Toss together with the onions and tomatoes and serve with risoni or your favourite pasta for a warming winter meal.
- Freshly made horseradish gremolata (basics) is wonderful to throw over any lamb or fish dish. For lamb, add a few finely chopped mint leaves for a little extra twist.

fennel and tomato salad

tang

Lime and lemon grass are the flavours that add zing to the cuisines of South-East Asia. Just think of the heady aromatics that fill the air as finely chopped lemon grass hits the hot metal of a wok, the delicate flavour of richly green lime leaves and fresh lime juice's startling tang. With their dimpled skin, the curious looking makrut or kaffir limes impart a wonderful citrusy edge to curries and the like. Grind their finely chopped glossy dark green leaves into a paste and savour their delight with spiced fish or salmon and lime fishcakes. But the tall, pale green stems of lemon grass are perhaps the most subtle members of the tang dynasty. Today, their delicate lemon fragrance is just as at home wafting around the kitchens of the western world as it is in Asia.

steamed chicken with cashew nut and mint salad

mango and coconut chutney

steamed chicken with cashew nut and mint salad

3 tablespoons lime juice
1 teaspoon sugar
2 tablespoons olive oil
1 lime, peeled
1 lemon grass stalk, trimmed and base removed, roughly chopped
2 garlic cloves
1 tablespoon grated fresh ginger
1 large red chilli, seeded and roughly chopped
1 1/2 tablespoons fish sauce
1/4 teaspoon ground white pepper
4 x 200 g (7 oz) chicken breast fillets
200 g (7 oz) bean sprouts
25 g (1/2 bunch) Vietnamese mint, leaves picked
80 g (1/2 cup) roughly chopped roast cashews

To make the dressing, combine the lime juice, sugar and olive oil in a bowl. Put the lime peel, lemon grass, garlic, ginger, chilli, fish sauce and white pepper in a food processor and process into a paste. Rub over the chicken before placing in a steamer basket over a pot of boiling water for 20 minutes. Toss the sprouts and mint together and put on a serving platter. Slice the chicken across the grain and arrange over the salad. Scatter with cashews and drizzle with the dressing. Serve with steamed rice. Serves 4

mango and coconut chutney

90 g (1 cup) desiccated coconut
1 large green chilli, seeded and roughly chopped
1 teaspoon finely grated fresh ginger
1 teaspoon lime juice
5 tablespoons natural yoghurt
60 g (1/3 cup) finely diced mango
2 tablespoons vegetable oil
2 teaspoons mustard seeds
4 small sprigs curry leaves

Put the coconut, chilli and ginger in a food processor or blender and process into a fine paste. Transfer the mixture to a small bowl and add the lime juice, yoghurt and mango.

In a small frying pan, heat the oil over a medium heat and, when hot, add the mustard seeds and curry leaves. When the mustard seeds begin to pop, remove from the heat and spoon the seeds over the coconut mixture. Drain the curry leaves on paper towels.

Stir the warm mustard seeds into the coconut mixture and spoon into a small serving bowl. Garnish with the curry leaves and serve with the lime prawns on page 56. Serves 4 as a side dish

avocado with chilli salsa

2 avocados
2 limes
1 tablespoon finely chopped red onion
8 cherry tomatoes, finely chopped
1 red chilli, seeded and finely chopped
1 tablespoon finely chopped coriander (cilantro) leaves
2 tablespoons extra virgin olive oil
1 teaspoon smoky paprika
1 handful coriander (cilantro) leaves
4 small corn tortillas, toasted over a flame or baked

Slice the avocados in half lengthways. Remove the seed and scoop out the whole flesh with a large spoon. Put the avocados face down onto a plate and finely slice to form a fan. Squeeze half a lime over each avocado half and season with sea salt and freshly ground black pepper. Combine the onion, tomato, chilli and chopped coriander in a bowl then sprinkle over the avocado. Finish off with a drizzle of olive oil and a sprinkle of paprika. Garnish with the coriander leaves and serve with the toasted tortillas. Serves 4 as a starter

fresh and fast

- Fresh Indian chutneys, like salsas, are a wonderful way to add a bit of spice to a meal. If you are not a fan of mango then substitute diced green papaya or cucumber in the mango and coconut chutney recipe.
- The crust on the steamed chicken is also beautiful on salmon or blue-eye cod. Rub the paste over the fish and steam or bake until the fillets are cooked through. Serve with an Asian vegetable salad or baby leaf green salad.
- Finely chop avocado and toss with lime juice, chillies, coriander (cilantro), cucumber and quartered cherry tomatoes. Season and spoon over grilled fish and drizzle with extra virgin olive oil.
- Bean sprouts have a very short shelf life and really need to be used on the day they are bought. If you have the time and are not using too many, it is nice to top and tail them, leaving just the white crunchy stem. If you are left with a large amount that needs using, rinse them under running water, roughly chop them and stir-fry with a little oyster sauce and chilli. Garnish with fresh lime and serve as a side dish.

avocado with chilli salsa

salmon with lemon grass and black vinegar dressing

1 lemon grass stalk
1 tablespoon finely grated fresh ginger
6 tablespoons mirin
2 tablespoons Chinese black vinegar
500 g (1 bunch) English spinach, washed and trimmed
4 spring onions (scallions), trimmed and cut into 3 cm (1 1/4 in) lengths
4 x 180 g (6 oz) salmon fillets

To make the lemon grass and black vinegar dressing, trim the lemon grass stalk of its tough outer leaves and base. Slice the stalk in half lengthways and finely chop the tender bottom 3 cm (1 1/4 in). Put in a small bowl with the ginger, mirin and vinegar.

Put the English spinach leaves and spring onions in a large frying pan. Add 250 ml (1 cup) of water and top with the salmon. Place over a high heat and cover so that the water begins to steam the spinach. Cook for a further 8 minutes.

Remove the salmon carefully and place onto warmed plates with the spinach and spring onions. Spoon over the dressing. Season with freshly ground black pepper. Serves 4

spiced fish

2 garlic cloves
3 cm (1 1/4 in) piece galangal, peeled and chopped
3 small red chillies, seeded and chopped
3 cm (1 1/4 in) piece of ginger, peeled and chopped
2 lemon grass stalks, trimmed and chopped
15 macadamia nuts
2 tablespoons olive oil
2 red onions, peeled and finely sliced
8 makrut (kaffir lime) leaves
1 x 400 ml (14 fl oz) can coconut milk
2 tomatoes, diced
600 g (1 lb 5 oz) ling or similar firm white fish, cut into large chunks
80 g (1 bunch) coriander (cilantro)
steamed rice

Put the garlic, galangal, chillies, ginger, lemon grass and macadamia nuts into a food processor or blender and process until a thick paste forms.

Heat the olive oil in a frying pan over a medium heat and add the onion and makrut leaves. Cook until the onions are soft. Add the spice paste and stir until aromatic. Add the coconut milk, tomatoes and fish then simmer for 8 minutes. Season to taste with sea salt and freshly ground black pepper. Garnish with coriander sprigs and serve with steamed rice. Serves 4

spinach and watercress stir-fry

1 tablespoon vegetable oil
2 tablespoons finely chopped lemon grass
1 small red chilli, seeded and finely chopped
2 red capsicums (peppers), finely sliced
90 g (1/2 cup) tinned water chestnuts, roughly chopped
500 g (1 lb 2 oz) English spinach, finely sliced
400 g (1 bunch) watercress, tough stems removed
1 tablespoon light soy sauce
1 teaspoon brown sugar
1 tablespoon fish sauce

Heat the oil in a wok or large frying pan over a medium to high heat. Add the lemon grass and chilli and cook for 1 minute before adding the capsicum. Cook the capsicum for a further minute before adding the water chestnuts, spinach and watercress. Stir-fry for 1 minute or so until the leaves are beginning to wilt and then add the soy sauce, sugar and fish sauce. Toss together and serve immediately with steamed jasmine rice or slippery white noodles. Serves 4

chipotle chicken

1 teaspoon all spice
1/2 teaspoon cinnamon
1 teaspoon ground cumin
1 teaspoon ground coriander
1 tablespoon finely chopped tinned chipotle chilli
2 tablespoons fresh oregano leaves
4 tablespoons olive oil
2 tablespoons lime juice
4 chicken drumsticks
4 chicken thighs
1 orange, zested and juiced
1 x 400 g (14 oz) can tomatoes
2 green capsicums (peppers), cut into thick chunks
couscous (basics)
20 green olives, pitted and roughly chopped

Put the all spice, cinnamon, cumin, coriander, chipotle chilli, oregano, olive oil and lime juice into a large bowl and stir. Add the chicken and toss until well coated. Cover and put in the fridge to marinate for a couple of hours or overnight. Heat a large frying pan over a high heat, add the chicken and cook until golden brown. Set aside on paper towels. Drain any excess fat from the pan and add the orange zest and juice, tomato, capsicum and chicken. Cover and simmer for 30 minutes. Serve on a bed of couscous with a garnish of green olives. Serves 4

asian-style vegetable salad

lime leaf chicken

4 x 200 g (7 oz) chicken breast fillets
8 makrut (kaffir lime) leaves
2 tablespoons shaved palm sugar
1 garlic clove
2 teaspoons fish sauce
15 mint leaves
3 tablespoons olive oil
250 g (9 oz) sugar snap peas, blanched and sliced on the diagonal
steamed rice

Slice the chicken breasts into four pieces lengthways and put in a bowl. Using a pair of kitchen scissors, finely cut the makrut leaves and put them into a food processor or blender with the palm sugar, garlic, fish sauce, mint leaves and olive oil. Process for 1 minute. Pour the marinade over the chicken and stir so the chicken is well coated. Cover and put in the fridge to marinate for 1 hour or overnight. Heat a non-stick frying pan or barbecue and cook the chicken pieces for a few minutes each side. Serve with the sugar snap peas and steamed rice. Serves 4

asian-style vegetable salad

1 teaspoon sambal oelek
1 tablespoon finely chopped lemon grass
3 tablespoons lime juice
1 tablespoon palm sugar
1 tablespoon finely chopped mint
300 g (10 1/2 oz) French beans, trimmed and cut in half
1 red capsicum (pepper), julienned
90 g (1 cup) bean sprouts
1 Lebanese (short) cucumber, julienned
8 cm (3 in) piece daikon radish, peeled and finely julienned
1 carrot, peeled and finely julienned
40 g (1/4 cup) finely chopped roast peanuts

To make the dressing, put the sambal oelek, lemon grass, lime juice, palm sugar and mint into a small bowl and stir to combine.

Blanch the beans in boiling water until they are dark green then drain and rinse under running cold water. Put them into a bowl with all the remaining ingredients, except the peanuts, and toss together. Pour over the dressing, toss the salad and allow to sit for 15 minutes before serving. Garnish with the peanuts and serve with any simple rice-based dish. Serves 6 as a side dish

lime and cashew blue-eye cod rolls with black vinegar

120 g (1 cup) salted and roasted cashews
1 large red chilli, seeded and roughly chopped
1 handful coriander (cilantro) leaves
1 teaspoon finely grated lime zest
1 tablespoon lime juice
500 g (1 lb 2 oz) blue-eye cod fillets, divided into 12 portions
12 small rice paper wrappers
2 tablespoons peanut oil
2 tablespoons Chinese black vinegar or balsamic vinegar

Put the cashews, chilli, coriander, lime zest and juice into a food processor or blender and process into a paste. Put 1 tablespoon of cashew paste on the top of each fish piece and set aside. Dip one of the rice paper wrappers in a bowl of water until it has softened. Place on a dry surface and put the fish on top. Fold the wrapper around the fish to form a neat parcel. Set aside and repeat with the remaining fish.

Heat half the oil in a non-stick frying pan over a medium heat and begin to cook the fish parcels. Cook for 3 minutes on each side, or until golden brown. You may wish to add more oil when necessary. Serve with the vinegar as a dipping sauce. Serves 4 as a starter

fresh and fast

- Chinese black vinegar can be bought in Asian supermarkets and is a wonderful kitchen essential to have on hand. Its rich flavour makes it a great dipping sauce as well as a basic for easy sauces. If you can't find it, use a lightly sweetened balsamic vinegar instead.
- Combine 3 tablespoons of lime juice with 1 tablespoon of shaved palm sugar, 1 teaspoon of fish sauce, some finely chopped lemon grass and coriander (cilantro) and pour over freshly barbecued prawns (shrimp) or fish.
- Use rice paper wrappers to make easy barbecue finger food. Wrap your favourite ingredients in softened wrappers and sear on a well oiled chargrill pan (griddle). Allow to cool slightly before passing around with a bowl of Chinese black vinegar or Vietnamese dipping sauce (basics).
- Makrut (kaffir lime) leaves make a wonderful marinade base for seafood or chicken. The easiest way to slice them finely is with a pair of kitchen scissors. Simply snip the leaves into a bowl and add some finely chopped chilli, lime juice and olive oil. Toss prawns (shrimp), fish fillets or chicken pieces in the marinade and leave for several hours or overnight.

lime and cashew blue-eye cod rolls with black vinegar

salmon and lime fishcake

Luscious emerald-green limes bring a tangy bite to any dish.

salmon and lime fishcakes

6 makrut (kaffir lime) leaves, 2 very finely sliced and chopped
500 g (1 lb 2 oz) salmon fillet, skin removed and boned
160 g (2 cups) fresh breadcrumbs
2 tablespoons finely chopped coriander (cilantro) leaves
2 tablespoons very finely chopped lemon grass
2 large red chillies, seeded and finely chopped
30 g (1/2 cup) finely sliced spring onions (scallions)
2 eggs
1 teaspoon fish sauce
1 tablespoon lime juice
1/2 teaspoon ground white pepper
80 ml (1/3 cup) vegetable oil
2 limes, halved
green salad

Put 250 ml (1 cup) of water and 4 makrut leaves into a frying pan over a high heat. Add the salmon then reduce the heat and simmer, covered, for 5 minutes, or until cooked through.

Using a fork, break up the cooled salmon and combine in a bowl with the breadcrumbs, sliced makrut leaves, coriander, lemon grass, chillies, spring onions, eggs, fish sauce, lime juice and white pepper. Shape into 12 patties. Heat some oil in a non-stick frying pan over a medium heat and cook the fishcakes, in batches, until they are golden brown. Add oil to the pan as you need it. Serve with lime halves and a green salad. Serves 4

vietnamese beef soup

2 litres (8 cups) beef stock
1 lemon grass stalk, crushed
1/4 teaspoon Chinese five-spice powder
1 tablespoon finely grated fresh ginger
2 red onions, peeled and finely sliced
180 g (6 oz) dried rice vermicelli
400 g (14 oz) rump steak, semi frozen and thinly sliced
3 tablespoons fish sauce
80 g (1 bunch) mint
90 g (1 bunch) coriander (cilantro)
50 g (1 bunch) Vietnamese mint

Put the stock, lemon grass, five-spice powder, ginger and onion into a large pot over a high heat and bring to the boil. Reduce the heat and simmer for 10 minutes. Place the rice vermicelli into a large bowl and cover with boiling water. Soak for 5 minutes, then drain and set aside.

Add the steak and fish sauce to the soup and simmer for 1 minute. Divide the noodles between four bowls then ladle over the hot soup, removing the lemon grass stalk. Add a handful of mixed herbs to each bowl and serve immediately. Serves 4

aromatic noodles with seared salmon

200 g (7 oz) buckwheat (soba) noodles
2 tablespoons olive oil
4 x 180 g (6 oz) salmon fillets
1 teaspoon sesame oil
1 tablespoon finely grated fresh ginger
2 garlic cloves, crushed
2 large red chillies, seeded and finely chopped
4 spring onions (scallions), finely sliced
1 teaspoon lime juice
1 tablespoon soy sauce
1 teaspoon fish sauce
30 g (1 bunch) garlic chives, chopped into 2 cm (3/4 in) lengths

Bring a large pot of water to the boil and cook the noodles until they are *al dente*. Drain and rinse under cold running water.

Heat a large frying pan or wok over a high heat and add half the olive oil. When the oil is hot, add the salmon, skin side down, and cook for 1 minute. Turn and cook for another 2 minutes before removing from the pan. Drain the oil and return the pan to the heat. Add the sesame oil and remaining olive oil. Add the ginger, garlic, chillies, spring onions, lime juice, soy and fish sauces. Stir-fry for 1 minute and then add the noodles, tossing until they are well coated. Remove from the heat and add the chives. Toss again, then divide the noodles between four bowls and top with the salmon. Serves 4

prawns with tomato sauce

2 tablespoons olive oil
5 garlic cloves, thinly sliced
5 spring onions (scallions), peeled and thinly sliced
5 makrut (kaffir lime) leaves
5 vine-ripened tomatoes, finely chopped
20 g (1/2 oz) palm sugar, shaved
4 tablespoons lime juice
1 tablespoon fish sauce
20 large raw prawns (shrimp), peeled, deveined and tails intact

To make the tomato sauce, heat the oil in a saucepan over a medium heat and cook the garlic and spring onions until golden brown. Add the makrut leaves and tomatoes and simmer for about 5 minutes, or until the tomatoes are soft. Add the sugar, lime juice and fish sauce and simmer for another 10 minutes. Remove from the heat.

Heat a non-stick frying pan over a high heat and sear the prawns for approximately 2 to 3 minutes, or until pink on both sides and beginning to curl up. Serve with the tomato sauce. Serves 4

seared salmon with green mango salad

2 tablespoons tamarind purée
2 tablespoons finely grated fresh ginger
1 tablespoon olive oil
4 x 100 g (3 1/2 oz) salmon fillets
60 ml (1/4 cup) lime juice
3 tablespoons fish sauce
3 tablespoons sugar
2 green mangoes
4 handfuls snow pea sprouts

Put the tamarind purée, ginger and olive oil into a small bowl and stir to combine. Toss the salmon in the mixture and allow to marinate for 30 minutes.

To make the green mango salad, combine the lime juice, fish sauce and sugar in a bowl and stir until the sugar has dissolved. Peel the mangoes and finely julienne or grate the flesh. Add to the bowl with the dressing.

Heat a non-stick pan over a medium heat and cook the salmon pieces for 2 minutes each side. Serve with the salad and snow pea sprouts. Serves 4 as a starter

squid with chilli dressing

1 small red chilli, seeded and finely chopped
4 tablespoons rice wine vinegar
2 tablespoons extra virgin olive oil
1 teaspoon sesame oil
2 teaspoons caster (superfine) sugar
2 teaspoons fish sauce
1 tablespoon lime juice
1 tablespoon finely chopped mint
400 g (1 bunch) watercress, sprigs picked
130 g (1 cup) finely julienned daikon radish
600 g (1 lb 5 oz) baby squid, cleaned

To make the chilli dressing, put the chilli, rice wine vinegar, olive oil, sesame oil, sugar, fish sauce, lime juice and mint into a bowl and stir to combine. Toss the watercress sprigs and the daikon together in a bowl. Pile onto four small plates.

Score the surface of the squid tubes in a crisscross pattern with a sharp knife. Heat a non-stick frying pan over a high heat and cook the squid for 1 to 2 minutes, or until it is just white. Remove from the heat and slice into thick bite-sized pieces. Put into the bowl with the chilli dressing and toss until the squid is well coated. Place the squid pieces onto the salad and spoon over the remaining dressing. Serves 4 as a starter

roast pumpkin salad

roast chicken with lime pickle

1.8 kg (4 lb) free-range chicken
1 lemon, halved
1 onion, quartered
2 tablespoons butter
3 tablespoons Indian lime pickle, finely chopped
1 handful watercress sprigs
mashed potato (basics)

Preheat the oven to 200°C (400°F/Gas 6). Rinse the chicken and pat it dry with paper towels. Put the chicken on a baking tray, breast side up, and stuff with the lemon and onion. Push the butter under the skin of the chicken breast. Rub the lime pickle over the chicken and lightly season with sea salt. Bake for 1 hour 15 minutes, or until cooked through. Take out the chicken and check that it is cooked by pulling a leg away from the body — the juices that run out should be clear and not pink.

Allow the chicken to rest for 15 minutes before carving and serving on a platter. Drizzle with some of the pan juices and garnish with watercress sprigs. Serve with mashed potato or the tomato and spinach rice on page 147. Serves 4

roast pumpkin salad

2 red capsicums (peppers)
800 g (1 lb 12 oz) pumpkin, peeled
4 tablespoons olive oil
1 tablespoon finely chopped lemon grass
1 tablespoon lemon juice
1 teaspoon sesame oil
1 teaspoon shaved palm sugar
1 teaspoon soy sauce
100 g (3 1/2 oz) baby rocket (arugula) leaves

Preheat the oven to 180°C (350°F/Gas 4). Roast the capsicums until the skin is blistered or blackened and put into a bowl. Cover with plastic wrap and set aside. Chop the pumpkin into 8 large pieces and put on a baking tray. Rub with half the oil and place in the oven. Bake for 40 minutes, or until the pumpkin is cooked through. Meanwhile, peel and seed the capsicums then finely dice the flesh. Put in a bowl with the lemon grass, lemon juice, sesame oil, palm sugar, soy sauce and remaining olive oil. Stir to combine.

Serve the baked pumpkin on a bed of rocket leaves and spoon over the capsicum mixture. Season with freshly ground black pepper. Serves 4

sesame crisps with lime prawns

1 tablespoon finely chopped lemon grass
1 red chilli, seeded and finely chopped
2 tablespoons lime juice
3 tablespoons olive oil
16 large raw prawns (shrimp), shelled and deveined with tails intact
8 sesame crisps (basics)
80 g (1 bunch) coriander (cilantro)
4 tablespoons lemon mayonnaise (basics)

Put the lemon grass, chilli, lime juice and olive oil into a small bowl. Add the prawns to the bowl then cover and place in the fridge for several hours to marinate.

Meanwhile, prepare the sesame crisps and set aside. Heat a large non-stick frying pan over a medium heat. Add the prawns and cook for approximately 2 to 3 minutes or until they are pink and beginning to curl up.

To assemble, place a sesame crisp on each serving plate and top with the prawns, coriander sprigs, a large dollop of lemon mayonnaise and the remaining sesame crisps.
Serves 4 as a starter

fresh and fast

- Indian lime pickle is another great store cupboard secret. Finely chop and toss through couscous and garnish with fresh herb leaves for an easy side dish. Or finely chop the pickle and add it to diced cucumber and tomatoes then drizzle with a little oil and spoon over grilled fish or chicken.
- There is nothing nicer than the combination of prawns and fresh lime. Toss prawns in a mixture of lime juice, paprika, fresh coriander and a little olive oil. Allow to marinate for several hours or overnight and then lightly grill (broil). The prawns will need little cooking as the lime juice will have partially "cooked" them already.
- Fried won ton wrappers make great party food. Fry them without the sesame seed coating and serve with simple toppings. Or season the egg wash with sea salt, black pepper and chilli flakes for won tons with a bit of bite.
- Toss pumpkin pieces in a little soy sauce with some finely chopped lemon grass, lime juice and olive oil. Bake until golden brown and serve with roast chicken.

sesame crisps with lime prawns

seasoned

Not everything is black and white. You just need to look at the silver-grey grains of the misnamed 'white pepper' to see that there is more to seasoning than the sublime snowy flakes of sea salt. But, when it comes down to it, salt and pepper are one of the most common — and important — pairings in the food world. Consider that salad of sweet red tomatoes without a generous scatter of crystal white flakes or grilled meat without a healthy bite of freshly ground black pepper. From kitchen table seasonings to the rich saltiness of capers, anchovies and olives or the sublime piquancy of pink peppercorns to the tongue-numbing zap of the Sichuan peppercorn — these seasonings are at the heart of good food. Let's face it, it's hard to imagine a culinary life without them.

whiting fillets with herbed butter

wilted spinach salad

whiting fillets with herb butter

1 handful flat-leaf (Italian) parsley leaves
2 tablespoons chopped chives
1 garlic clove, chopped
2 gherkins, chopped
3 anchovy fillets
1 tablespoon salted capers
1/4 teaspoon white pepper
100 g (3 1/2 oz) butter, softened
1 teaspoon olive oil
8 whiting fillets (about 500 g/1 lb 2 oz)
400 g (1 bunch) watercress, sprigs picked

Put the parsley, chives, garlic, gherkin, anchovies, capers, white pepper and butter into a food processor or blender and process until a smooth paste forms. Lay a large piece of plastic wrap on a clean surface and spoon the flavoured butter in a line. Roll up to form a log and refrigerate until you are ready to use it.

Heat the olive oil in a large non-stick frying pan over a high heat. Cook the whiting for 1 to 2 minutes on each side, then remove from the pan. Serve on a bed of watercress topped with a few slices of the herbed butter. Serves 4

wilted spinach salad

1 kg (2 bunches) English spinach, rinsed and stalks removed
12 Kalamata olives, pitted and roughly chopped
1 garlic clove, finely chopped
2 tablespoons finely chopped mint leaves
1 small red onion, halved and finely sliced
2 tablespoons red wine vinegar
200 g (7 oz) feta cheese, crumbled
6 tablespoons olive oil
30 g (1 cup) croutons

Make sure the spinach is well drained before roughly chopping the larger leaves and placing into a large metal bowl. Add the olives, garlic, mint, onion and vinegar then crumble the feta cheese over. Heat the olive oil in a frying pan over a high heat until it is almost smoking then pour it over the salad. Be careful to stand well back as some of the oil may splatter. Toss the ingredients one more time and pile them into a serving bowl. Scatter with croutons and serve immediately. Serves 4 as a side dish

fig and goat's cheese salad with a sichuan dressing

1 teaspoon Sichuan peppercorns, crushed
1 teaspoon honey
1/2 tablespoon balsamic vinegar
3 tablespoons olive oil
1–2 butter lettuce
8 ripe figs, quartered
200 g (7 oz) soft goat's cheese

To make the Sichuan dressing, put the peppercorns, honey, vinegar and olive oil into a small bowl and stir until the honey has dissolved. Make the salad by arranging the smallest leaves of the lettuce on four salad plates. Divide the figs between the plates and crumble the goat's cheese over. Drizzle with the dressing and serve with a crusty baguette. Serves 4

fresh and fast

- Herbed butters are a great way to flavour food with little fuss. Better still, they can be stored in the fridge or freezer for use at any time. Try peppery basil and sundried tomato butter for grilled steaks, or fresh horseradish and mustard. A buttery blend of lime zest and coriander is wonderful with grilled (broiled) fish, as are dill and capers.
- Stuff ripe figs with a little goat's cheese, wrap in prosciutto and bake in a hot oven for a few minutes. Serve on a bed of greens with a drizzle of olive oil and balsamic vinegar.
- Blend feta cheese, olives and a little cream together to create a flavour-packed spread for bruschetta. Top with a scatter of torn basil or thyme and finely sliced tomato, fig or pear.
- Marinate chunks of goat's cheese overnight in olive oil flavoured with peppercorns, bay leaves, thyme and lemon zest. Serve on a bed of rocket (arugula) leaves with croutons.

fig and goat's cheese salad with a sichuan dressing

polenta and zucchini salad with blue cheese dressing

75 g (1/2 cup) polenta
2 teaspoons butter
3 tablespoons olive oil
6 zucchini (courgettes), sliced on the diagonal
2 tablespoons blue cheese, crumbled
4 tablespoons extra virgin olive oil
1 tablespoon red wine vinegar
150 g (5 1/2 oz) baby English spinach leaves

Preheat the oven to 200°C (400°F/Gas 6). Bring 350 ml (1 1/3 cups) of salted water to the boil in a large saucepan. Slowly pour in the polenta and stir until the polenta thickens and begins to draw away from the sides of the saucepan. Stir in the butter then remove from the heat. Pour the polenta onto a tray or flat plate until 1 cm (1/2 in) thick. Allow to cool. Put the zucchini on a baking tray and brush with the olive oil. Bake until soft and cooked through. Slice the cooled polenta into rectangular chips and put on an oiled tray. Brush the polenta with a little oil and bake for 10 minutes.

To make the blue cheese dressing, combine the blue cheese, extra virgin olive oil and vinegar in a small bowl. Layer the zucchini, polenta and spinach onto four serving plates and drizzle with the dressing. Serves 4 as a starter

mustard rubbed tuna salad

1 teaspoon ground white pepper
1 tablespoon Dijon mustard
3 tablespoons olive oil
400 g (14 oz) tuna fillet, cut into 2 cm (3/4 in) square lengths
400 g (1 bunch) watercress, leaves picked
70 g (1 bunch) chervil, trimmed
2 small zucchini (courgettes), finely sliced
4 red radishes, finely sliced
125 g (1/2 cup) lemon mayonnaise (basics)

Mix the white pepper, Dijon mustard and 1 tablespoon of olive oil together in a small bowl. Rub the mustard mixture all over the tuna. Add the remaining olive oil to a large non-stick frying pan and heat over a high heat. Sear the tuna for 1 minute on each side. Remove from the heat and allow to rest. Divide the watercress, chervil, zucchini and radish between four plates. Cut the tuna fillet into thin slices and arrange over the salad. Top with a dollop of lemon mayonnaise. Serves 4 as a starter

eggplant relish with chicken

4 tablespoons olive oil
10 small Japanese eggplants (aubergines), sliced in half lengthways
4 red onions, finely sliced
4 garlic cloves, finely sliced
3 tablespoons red wine vinegar
4 tablespoons lemon juice
3 tablespoons brown sugar
2 teaspoons white peppercorns, lightly crushed
30 g (1 cup) coriander (cilantro) leaves
4 single chicken breast fillets

Preheat the oven to 200°C (400°F/Gas 6). Heat the olive oil in a frying pan over a medium to high heat. Fry the eggplant until it is golden brown. Remove and put in a large bowl. Add the onions and garlic and, reducing the heat, stir-fry until the onions are soft. Add to the eggplant. Put the vinegar, lemon juice, sugar and peppercorns into a saucepan and heat over a medium heat until the sugar has dissolved. Bring to the boil and pour the hot mixture over the eggplant and onion. Stir to combine and add the coriander when the relish is cool.

Meanwhile, heat a large frying pan over a high heat and sear the chicken until golden brown on both sides. Transfer to a baking tray and cover with foil. Bake for 15 minutes or until cooked through. Serve with the eggplant relish on the side. Serves 4

eggplant and ricotta cheese penne

125 ml (1/2 cup) vegetable oil
1 large eggplant (aubergine), cut into 1 cm (1/2 in) cubes
2 garlic cloves, minced
1 onion, finely chopped
4 zucchini (courgettes), finely sliced
100 g (3 1/2 oz) fresh ricotta cheese
20 fresh basil leaves, torn
20 fresh oregano leaves
50 g (1 3/4 oz) grated Parmesan cheese
400 g (14 oz) penne
2 tablespoons extra virgin olive oil

Heat a frying pan over a high heat and add the vegetable oil. Fry the eggplant cubes until they are golden and soft. Remove with a slotted spoon and set aside to drain on paper towels. Pour off most of the oil, leaving a small amount just coating the pan. Add the garlic and onion and cook over a medium heat until the onion is transparent. Add the zucchini and cook until it is just beginning to soften. Put the eggplant, zucchini, ricotta, basil, oregano and Parmesan into a large bowl.

Meanwhile, bring a large pot of salted water to the boil. Add the penne and cook until it is *al dente*. Drain and add to the other ingredients. Season with sea salt and freshly ground black pepper. Serve immediately with a drizzle of extra virgin olive oil. Serves 4

seared beef slices with plum sauce & mint

tofu with a black bean sauce

2 tablespoons olive oil
1 tablespoon finely grated fresh ginger
2 garlic cloves, minced
1 teaspoon chilli powder
2 tablespoons salted black beans, rinsed and drained
3 tablespoons mirin
400 g (14 oz) hard tofu, cut into 2 cm (3/4 in) squares
6 zucchini (courgettes), trimmed and finely sliced on the diagonal
1 lemon, juiced
steamed rice

Put the olive oil in a large frying pan or wok and heat over a high heat. Add the ginger, garlic and chilli powder and stir-fry for 1 minute. Add the black beans, mirin and 125 ml (1/2 cup) of water. Reduce the heat to a simmer then add the tofu and season with black pepper. Cook for 5 minutes, then add the zucchini. Toss together and cook for a further 2 minutes before adding the lemon juice. Serve with steamed rice. Serves 4

seared beef slices with plum sauce and mint salad

4 tablespoons plum sauce
4 tablespoons olive oil
1 tablespoon balsamic vinegar
1/2 teaspoon ground Sichuan peppercorns
4 spring onions (scallions), finely sliced
400 g (14 oz) sirloin steak, trimmed
100 g (3 1/2 oz) bean sprouts
1 butter lettuce
80 g (1 bunch) mint, leaves picked
2 tablespoons finely chopped raw cashews

Put the plum sauce, olive oil, vinegar, ground Sichuan peppercorns and spring onions into a bowl. Stir to combine. Heat a frying pan over a high heat and sear the steak for 2 minutes on both sides. Remove from the heat and allow to rest in the pan. Divide the bean sprouts and butter lettuce between four plates. Top with a scatter of mint leaves. Finely slice the beef and lay it over the salad. Spoon over the plum sauce mixture and scatter with the cashews. Serve with a warm baguette. Serves 4

pissaladiere

4 tablespoons olive oil
4–5 large onions, peeled and finely sliced
1 teaspoon finely chopped fresh rosemary
1 teaspoon finely chopped fresh thyme
1 teaspoon caster (superfine) sugar
1 quantity pizza dough (basics)
12 anchovy fillets
16 black olives, pitted
12 fresh basil leaves

Preheat the oven 220°C (425°F/Gas 7). Heat a large frying pan over a medium heat and add the olive oil, onions, rosemary and thyme. Cover and cook over a low heat for 20 minutes, or until the onions are very soft. Add the sugar and cook for a further minute before setting aside.

Turn out the risen dough onto a floured surface and punch it down. Divide into four sections and roll out each piece to form a thin oval. Turn the edges over a little to form a slightly thicker crust. Put on a large oiled baking tray and cover the surface of the pizzas with the onions. Tear the anchovies and olives into small pieces and dot over the onions. Bake for 15 minutes. Remove from the oven and garnish with freshly torn basil leaves. Serves 4

fresh and fast

- Caramelized onions will fill your kitchen with the most wonderful aromas as they cook. Flavour with lots of thyme, a dash of vinegar, mustard and a large blob of butter and serve with grilled (broiled) steak. Spread a little over toasted rye bread and top with slices of leg ham and Gruyère cheese for a ham and cheese melt with a difference.
- It's hard to beat a home-made pizza. Cover with your favourite toppings — richly fragrant tomato sauce, mozzarella, goat's cheese, fresh herbs, thinly sliced salami or anchovies — and bake to bubbling perfection.
- Marinate tofu overnight in a blend of soy sauce, palm sugar, a little sesame oil, spring onions, chilli and ginger. Serve sliced over steamed greens and rice.
- Fermented Chinese black beans are a great way to add an interesting salty flavour to many dishes. Toss a little with steamed greens and a splash of kecap manis or add to wok-fried hokkien noodles with finely sliced chillies and garlic chives.

roast tuna with fennel and tomato

A generous sprinkle of sea salt will perfectly complement a ripe tomato.

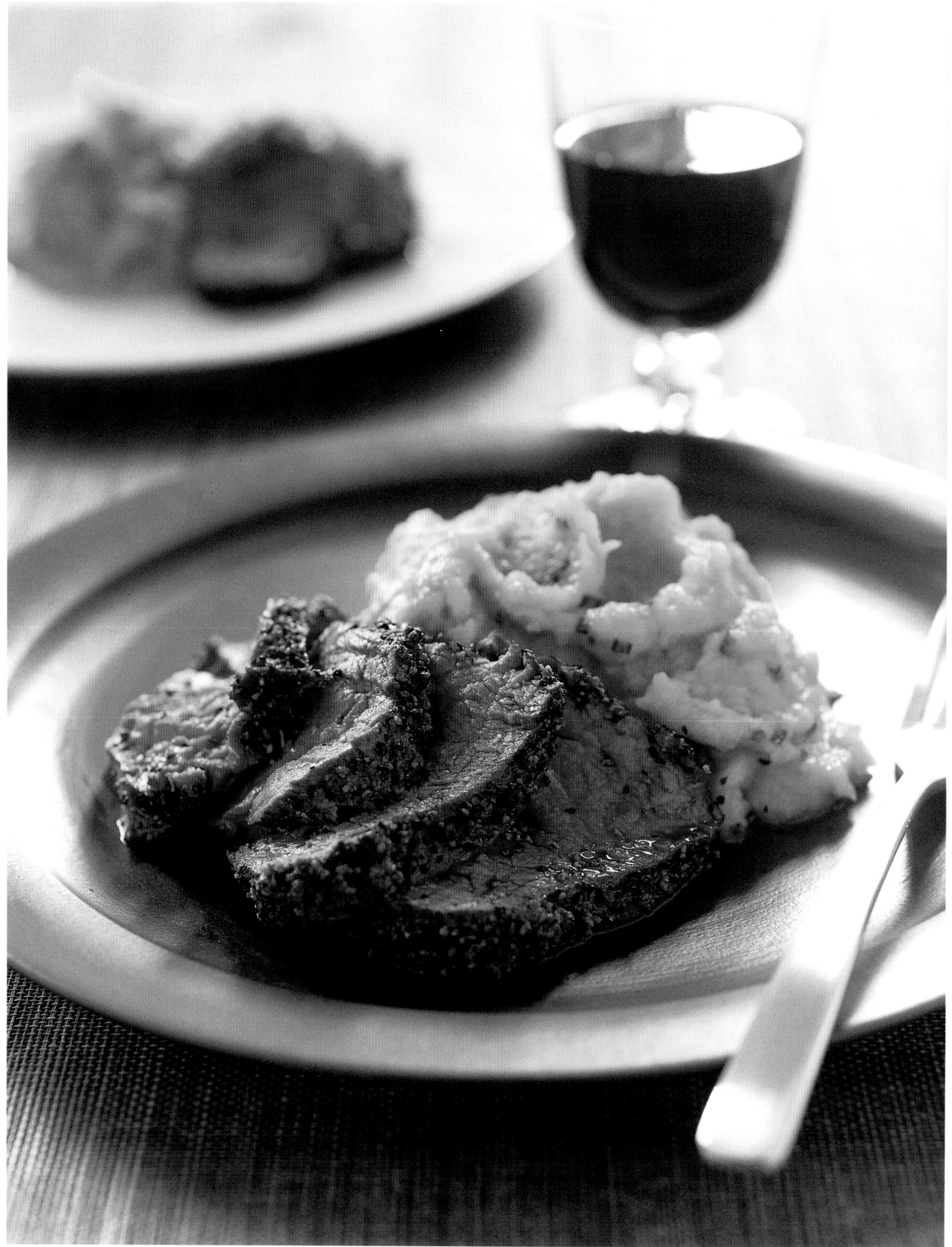

peppered beef with pumpkin mash

roast tuna with fennel and tomato

4 ripe tomatoes
2 garlic cloves, finely sliced
14–16 thyme sprigs
75 g (1/2 cup) small black olives
1 x 500 g (1 lb 2 oz) tuna fillet
2 tablespoons freshly ground black pepper
125 ml (1/2 cup) olive oil
15 basil leaves, roughly torn
1 fennel bulb, sliced paper thin
2 tablespoons extra virgin olive oil

Preheat the oven to 200°C (400°F/Gas 6). Bring a large pot of salted water to the boil. Make a small X-shaped incision at the base of each tomato and put in the boiling water for 1 minute. Remove with a slotted spoon and put in a bowl to cool.

Lay the garlic and thyme over the base of a small deep baking tray or cake tin and scatter with the olives. Roll the tuna fillet in the ground black pepper and place over the thyme in the baking tray. Drizzle with the olive oil and season with sea salt. Seal the baking tray with foil and bake in the oven for 25 to 30 minutes.

Meanwhile, peel the tomatoes and put them in a large bowl. Using a small sharp knife, roughly chop them while still in the bowl into bite-sized pieces. Season with sea salt and add the basil leaves. Toss to combine. Remove the tuna from the oven — it should be nicely pink in the middle. Remove the olives from the baking tray and add them to the tomato mixture along with 1 or 2 tablespoons of the cooking liquid. On a serving plate, layer the fennel with the tomato. Top with several thin slices of tuna, drizzle with extra virgin olive oil and garnish with thyme sprigs from the baking tray. Serves 4

peppered beef with pumpkin mash

1.5 kg (3 lb 5 oz) beef eye fillet
2 tablespoons freshly ground black pepper
1 kg (2 lb 4 oz) pumpkin
150 g (5 1/2 oz) butter
2 garlic cloves, minced
30 g (1 bunch) chives, finely chopped

Trim the fillet then rub the pepper into the surface. Put it on a tray and leave it in the fridge, uncovered, overnight.

Preheat the oven to 200°C (400°F/Gas 6). Put the fillet in a baking tray and roast for 10 minutes before turning the meat and cooking for a further 5 minutes. Remove from the oven and season the fillet with sea salt. Cover with foil and rest for 15 minutes. Drain any juices from the pan and retain them to pour over the meat later.

Meanwhile, peel the pumpkin and cut it into small pieces. Put it into a large saucepan with salted cold water and bring to the boil. Cook until tender. Melt the butter in a small saucepan over a medium heat. Add the garlic and chives then simmer for a few minutes. When the pumpkin is cooked, drain and mash. Stir in the butter mixture and whip to a fluffy mash. Cover and set aside in a warm place. Return the fillet to the oven for a further 15 minutes. Serve in thick slices with a drizzle of pan juices and a large spoonful of mashed pumpkin. Serves 6

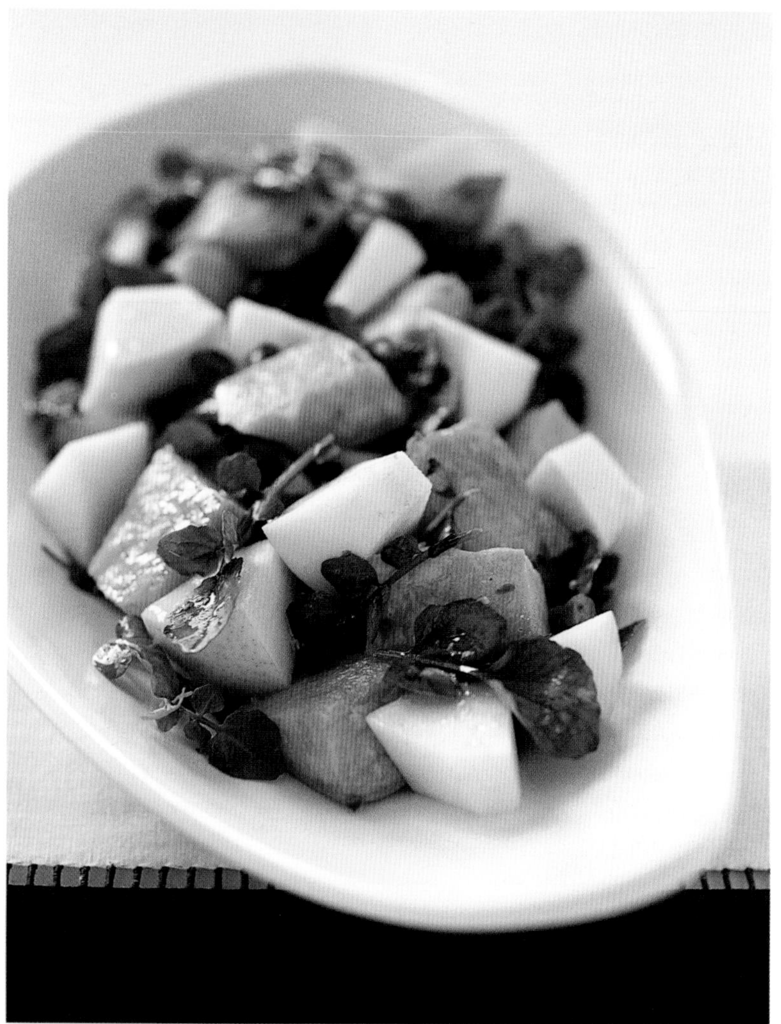

zucchini and sugar snap salad

200 g (7 oz) sugar snap peas, trimmed
4 zucchini (courgettes), trimmed and thickly sliced
6–8 radishes, trimmed and finely sliced
1 tablespoon lemon juice
3 tablespoons walnut oil
1 teaspoon celery salt
2 tablespoons toasted pepitas (pumpkin seeds)

Bring a pot of salted water to the boil. Add the sugar snap peas and blanch until they are bright green. Remove with a slotted spoon and rinse under running cold water. Add the zucchini to the boiling water and cook for 2 minutes. Put the zucchini and sugar snap peas in a large bowl with the radishes. To make the dressing, put the lemon juice, walnut oil, celery salt and some freshly ground black pepper into a small bowl and stir to combine. Drizzle the dressing over the salad and scatter toasted pepitas over the top. Serves 4 as a side salad.

blue-eye cod with white pepper and lemon sauce

2 lemons, juiced
1 teaspoon ground white pepper
1 teaspoon caster (superfine) sugar
4 x 200 g (7 oz) blue-eye cod fillets
2 tablespoons olive oil
3 vine-ripened tomatoes, roughly chopped
12 basil leaves

To make the white pepper and lemon sauce, put the lemon juice, white pepper and sugar into a small bowl and stir until the sugar has dissolved.

Rinse the fish fillets in cold water and dry on paper towels. Heat the olive oil in a large non-stick frying pan over a high heat. Add the fillets and cook for 2 minutes on one side. Turn the fish over and reduce the heat to low to medium. Cook for a further 3 to 4 minutes. Toss the tomato and basil together and divide between four plates. Arrange the fish over the top and spoon over the dressing. Serve with a rocket (arugula) salad. Serves 4

sweet potato, watercress and pear salad

1 large orange sweet potato (kumara)
2 tablespoons olive oil
1 lemon, juiced
1 tablespoon pink peppercorns, drained and finely chopped
3 tablespoons extra virgin olive oil
2 ripe green pears, quartered and cut into bite-sized pieces
400 g (1 bunch) watercress, sprigs picked

Preheat the oven to 180°C (350°F/Gas 4). Peel and cut the sweet potato into bite-sized pieces and put on a baking tray. Rub the pieces with 2 tablespoons of olive oil and season with a little sea salt. Bake for 30 minutes, or until they are golden brown and cooked through.

Meanwhile, put the lemon juice, peppercorns and extra virgin olive oil into a large bowl and stir to combine. Add the pear pieces and watercress and toss together. Arrange the pear salad on a serving plate then add the cooked sweet potato. Serves 4

pan-fried barramundi with lemon and black bean sauce

1 tablespoon olive oil
2 spring onions (scallions), trimmed and finely sliced
1 red capsicum (pepper), finely diced
2 tablespoons salted black beans, rinsed and drained
250 ml (1 cup) fish stock
1 lemon, juiced
1 tablespoon plain (all-purpose) flour
4 x 160 g (5¾ oz) barramundi fillets
125 ml (½ cup) peanut oil
steamed greens and rice

To make the lemon and black bean sauce, heat the olive oil in a frying pan over a medium heat and add the spring onions and capsicum. Cook for 5 minutes, or until the capsicum is soft. Add the black beans and stock and cook until reduced by half. Add the lemon juice then pour into a small bowl. Wipe out the pan with paper towels.

Put the flour into a plastic bag with ½ teaspoon of sea salt and freshly ground black pepper. Add the fish fillets and toss until they are lightly coated with flour. Heat the peanut oil in the frying pan over a high heat. Add the fish and cook for 2 minutes, turn the fish over and reduce the heat to medium. Cook for a further 5 minutes. Put the fish onto a serving plate and spoon over the sauce. Serve with steamed greens and rice. Serves 4

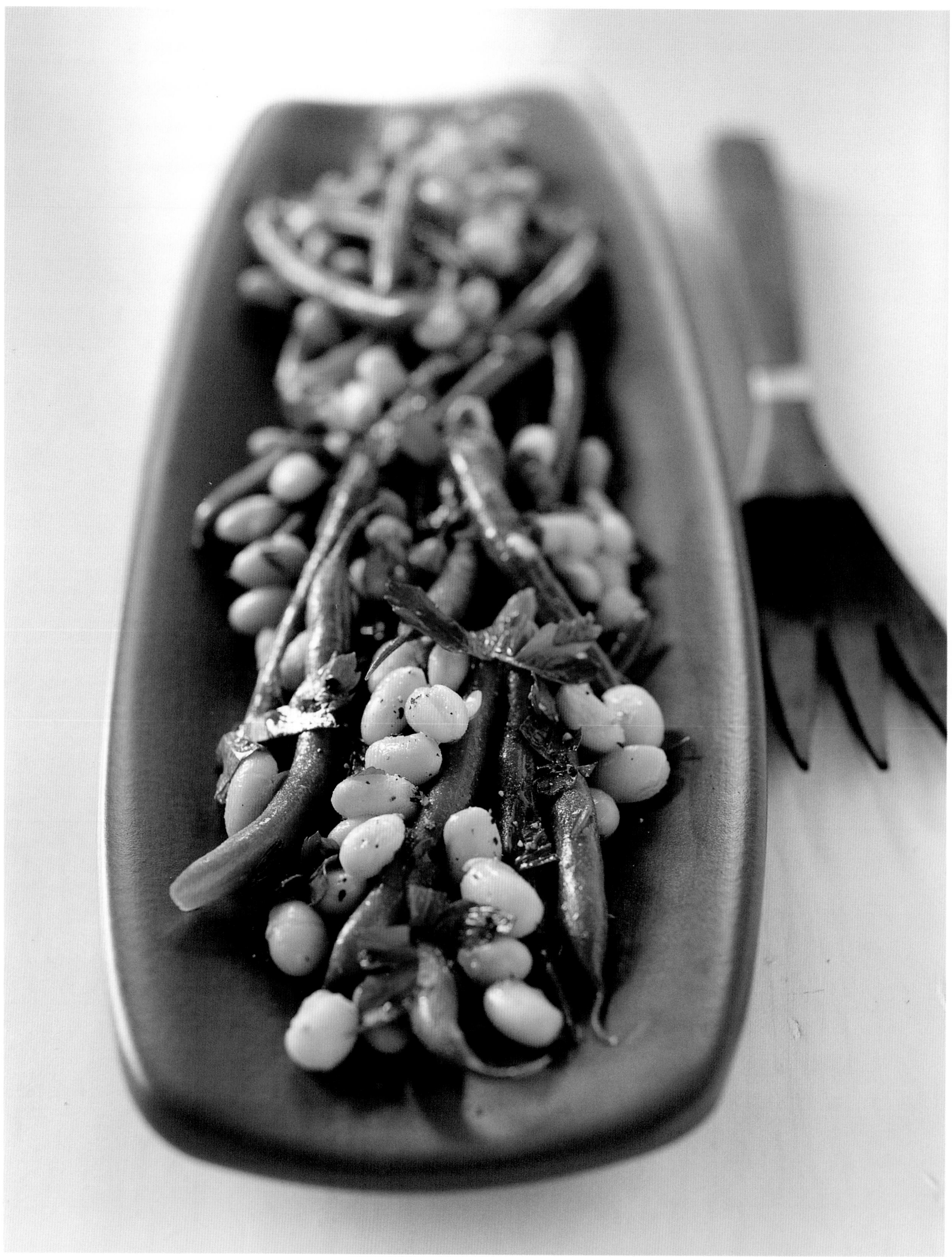

steak with onion salsa

bean salad

3 tablespoons extra virgin olive oil
1 tablespoon lemon juice
1 teaspoon walnut oil
1/2 teaspoon caster (superfine) sugar
1/2 teaspoon Dijon mustard
400 g (14 oz) green beans, trimmed
1 x 400 g (14 oz) can butter beans, drained and rinsed
1 handful chopped flat-leaf (Italian) parsley

Put the extra virgin olive oil, lemon juice, walnut oil, sugar and mustard into a large bowl and season liberally with freshly ground black pepper and sea salt. Whisk with a fork until combined. Blanch the green beans in boiling water until they begin to turn bright green then quickly drain and add to the bowl. Toss the green beans until they are well coated in the dressing. Allow to cool then add the butter beans and parsley and toss again. Serves 4 as a side dish

steak with onion salsa

2 large red onions, thickly sliced
2 ripe tomatoes
2 handfuls flat-leaf (Italian) parsley leaves
10 fresh oregano leaves
1 tablespoon balsamic vinegar
3 tablespoons extra virgin olive oil
4 x 180 g (6 oz) fillet steaks

Preheat a barbecue. To make the onion salsa, grill the onion until it is quite blackened on both sides. Remove and put on a chopping board. Put the tomatoes on the barbecue and, meanwhile, begin to roughly chop the cooked onion. Transfer the onion to a bowl. Once the tomatoes begin to blacken, turn them over and cook for a further minute. Put them in the bowl with the onions and roughly chop with a sharp knife or a pair of kitchen scissors. Add the parsley, oregano, vinegar and extra virgin olive oil. Season with sea salt and cracked black pepper to taste and toss all the salsa ingredients together.

Meanwhile, put the steaks on the barbecue and sear for 2 to 3 minutes. Turn over and cook for a further minute. Remove from the barbecue and set aside to rest. Serve with the onion salsa. Serves 4

snapper fillets with a pink peppercorn dressing

4 tablespoons olive oil
2 tablespoons lime juice
1 teaspoon pink peppercorns
1 tablespoon finely chopped pickled ginger
1 handful coriander (cilantro) leaves
1 tablespoon finely chopped lemon grass
4 x 200 g (7 oz) snapper fillets
2 tablespoons vegetable oil
steamed green beans, sliced on the diagonal

To make the pink peppercorn dressing, put the olive oil, lime juice, pink peppercorns, pickled ginger, coriander and lemon grass into a small bowl and stir to combine. Rinse the snapper fillets under running cold water and pat them dry with a paper towel. Season both sides of the fillets with sea salt. Heat the vegetable oil in a frying pan over a high heat and add the snapper skin side down. Using a spatula, press the surface of the fish into the hot pan and cook for 1 minute, or until the skin is crispy. Turn the fillets over, reduce the heat to medium and cook for a further 8 minutes.

Spoon the pink peppercorn dressing over the snapper and serve with steamed green beans. Serves 4

fresh and fast

- Add some chopped pink peppercorns to a dressing of olive oil, lemon juice and a little finely chopped basil. Drizzle over a salad of finely sliced orange, witlof, spinach leaves and steamed green beans.
- Canned butter beans are a store cupboard essential. Mash in a saucepan with a little butter and pepper and serve warm with grilled (broiled) lamb. Or blend with some heads of roast garlic, olive oil and finely chopped parsley. Serve on toasted sourdough bread with wild rocket (arugula) and shaved Parmesan cheese.
- To zest up the onion salsa, add some freshly ground cumin and chilli. Replace the oregano leaves with fresh coriander (cilantro) and serve with spicy sausages or grilled (broiled) lamb.
- Blanch French beans until they are emerald green. Drain and roughly chop before tossing in a bowl with butter, lemon juice, a little finely chopped rosemary and crushed garlic. Serve topped with freshly grilled (broiled) tuna and garnish with a scatter of small black olives.

snapper fillets with a pink peppercorn dressing

piquant

Piquant adj. Agreeably pungent, or sharp in taste or flavour; appetizing ... we could only be describing chilli and ginger, which bring an appetizing intensity to most dishes with their bursts of heat and bite. So many cultures have explored the fiery top notes of the chilli. From the ruby-red bird's eye, thinly sliced in South-East Asia, to the enriching heat of European paprika and on to the vast range of South American chillies, the chilli can never be called dull. Nor can its partner ginger, with its delicious aroma. An essential ingredient in Indian and North African cuisine, this pale gold wonder is one of the most versatile spices. In its powdered form, it brings the taste of the Orient to many a favourite cake or dessert, while freshly sliced slithers give a sweet heat to Asian-style salads. And what would Japanese food be without those fresh pale pink ribbons of pickled ginger to enhance a meal.

fresh lasagne with chilli crab

fresh lasagne with chilli crab

4 tablespoons olive oil
2 large red chillies, seeded and finely sliced
1/2 teaspoon smoky paprika
2 garlic cloves, minced
3 leeks, finely sliced
1 x 400 g (14 oz) tin chopped tomatoes
1 teaspoon caster (superfine) sugar
125 ml (1/2 cup) white wine
250 g (9 oz) crab meat
8 fresh lasagne sheets
70 g (2 1/2 oz) baby English spinach leaves
15 g (1/2 bunch) chives, cut into 3 cm (1 1/4 in) lengths

Bring a large pot of salted water to the boil. Heat the olive oil in a large pan over a medium heat and add the chillies, paprika and garlic. Cook for 1 minute before adding the leeks. Cover and simmer for 5 minutes, or until the leeks are soft. Add the tomatoes, 185 ml (3/4 cup) of water, sugar and wine. Simmer for a further 10 minutes. Season with sea salt and black pepper. Put the crab meat into a bowl and break up into fine threads with a fork.

Cook the lasagne in the boiling water until *al dente*. Add the crab meat to the tomato sauce. Drain the lasagne and put a sheet on a warmed plate. Spoon a little sauce onto half the sheet, add the spinach then fold. Repeat with the remaining ingredients, finishing off with the sauce and a sprinkle of chives. Serves 4

grilled mushrooms

8 field mushrooms
3 garlic cloves, finely chopped
1 teaspoon red chilli flakes
6 tablespoons extra virgin olive oil
8 slices ciabatta bread, toasted
150 g (1 bunch) rocket (arugula)
1 handful flat-leaf (Italian) parsley leaves

Put the mushrooms, stalk side up, on a baking tray. Combine the garlic, chillies and extra virgin olive oil in a small bowl. Spoon the flavoured oil over the mushrooms and season with a little sea salt. Place under a hot grill (broiler) and cook for 10 minutes. Remove from the heat. Put the toasted ciabatta onto four serving plates and add a few rocket leaves. Top with the warm mushrooms, scatter with the parsley leaves and drizzle with the cooking liquid. Serves 4 as a starter

cracked wheat salad

150 g (5 1/2 oz) cracked burghul wheat
60 g (2 1/4 oz) currants
2 tablespoons olive oil
2 large red onions, finely chopped
1/2 teaspoon ground cinnamon
1/2 teaspoon ground cardamom
1 teaspoon all spice
1 tablespoon grated fresh ginger
2 celery sticks, finely sliced
1 red chilli, seeded and finely sliced
200 g (7 oz) cooked chickpeas
60 g (2 1/4 oz) pine nuts, toasted
1 handful coriander (cilantro) leaves
1 handful flat-leaf (Italian) parsley leaves
10 mint leaves, roughly chopped

Put the burghul wheat and currants into a bowl and cover with 250 ml (1 cup) of boiling water. Heat the olive oil in a large saucepan over a medium heat. Add the onion, cinnamon, cardamom, all spice and ginger and cook until the onion is soft. Add the celery, chilli, chickpeas and pine nuts to the soaked burghul wheat and currants. Lightly fold the ingredients together in a bowl and season with sea salt and freshly ground black pepper.

Spoon into a serving bowl and add the fresh herbs. Serve as a light salad or with grilled chicken. Serves 4 to 6 as a side dish

fresh and fast

- Toss cooked crab meat with quartered cherry tomatoes, coriander (cilantro) leaves, finely chopped chilli, grated lime zest and a little good-quality mayonnaise. Serve with warm crusty bread and a baby leaf salad.
- Drizzle a little olive oil over large field mushrooms and grill (broil) for a few minutes. Spread with soft goat's curd and grill (broil) until lightly golden. Serve on toasted rye bread with a scatter of finely chopped walnuts.
- Pan-fry a selection of wild and button mushrooms in butter with a little crushed garlic. Add a little white wine and cream and simmer until the sauce has thickened. Cook several sheets of fresh lasagne and then layer with the mushrooms on serving plates. Top with a scatter of grated Parmesan cheese and lightly grill (broil). Serve with a drizzle of extra virgin olive oil and freshly ground black pepper.

cracked wheat salad

steamed fish with fresh ginger

4 perch fillets (about 500 g/1 lb 2 oz)
3 spring onions (scallions), finely sliced diagonally
4 cm (1 1/2 in) piece young ginger, finely julienned
80 ml (1/3 cup) peanut oil
lemon wedges

Bring a large pot of water to the boil then put a steamer basket on top. Steam the fish until it is cooked through. Meanwhile, put the spring onions and ginger in a metal bowl. Heat the peanut oil in a frying pan until it begins to smoke. Carefully pour the very hot oil over the ginger and spring onions and allow the oil to absorb the flavours. Place the fish on warm serving plates and spoon over the ginger oil. Serve with lemon wedges and steamed white rice. Serves 4

chilli beef on endive leaves

6 tablespoons peanut oil
6 cm (2 1/2 in) piece fresh ginger, peeled and julienned
500 g (1 lb 2 oz) lean beef mince
3 large red chillies, seeded and finely chopped
2 garlic cloves, crushed
1 teaspoon sesame oil
1 teaspoon balsamic vinegar
2 teaspoons soy sauce
4 tablespoons oyster sauce
10 basil leaves, finely sliced
4 whole witlof (chicory/Belgian endive), washed and leaves separated

Put the peanut oil into a frying pan and heat over a medium to high heat. Add the ginger to the oil and, once it begins to turn crisp and golden, remove and allow to drain on paper towels. Drain most of the oil, leaving just a little to coat the pan, and reduce the heat to medium. Add the mince, chilli, garlic and sesame oil to the hot pan and stir-fry until the meat is cooked and beginning to turn brown. Add the vinegar, soy sauce and oyster sauce and cook for a further 1 or 2 minutes before adding the basil leaves. Spoon the warm beef mixture into the endive leaves and top with the fried ginger. Serves 4 to 6 as a canapé

ginger duck and udon noodle broth

8 shiitake mushrooms
2 duck breast fillets
8 shallots, trimmed and sliced into 2 cm (3/4 in) lengths
2 tablespoons finely grated fresh ginger
200 g (7 oz) udon noodles
1 tablespoon dashi granules
4 tablespoons soy sauce
1 tablespoon sugar
200 g (7 oz) silken firm tofu, cut into 2 cm (3/4 in) cubes
2 tablespoons finely chopped garlic chives

Bring a pot of salted water to the boil. Meanwhile, put the mushrooms into a large bowl and cover with warm water. Soak for 10 minutes then remove the stalks and finely slice. Return the mushrooms to their soaking liquid. Trim the fatty skin from the duck and reserve. Cut the breast diagonally in very thin slices. Heat the duck fat in a frying pan over a medium heat, add the shallots, duck and ginger and sauté lightly for 4 to 5 minutes. Set aside and discard any fat.

Cook the noodles in the boiling water until *al dente* then rinse. Combine the dashi granules, soy sauce, sugar and 1.2 litres (42 fl oz) of water in a saucepan and bring to the boil. Reduce the heat, add the mushrooms and their strained soaking liquid and simmer for 10 minutes. Add the duck, shallots, ginger and tofu. Cook for 1 minute. Divide the noodles between four bowls, ladle over the broth and sprinkle with chives. Serves 4

chicken curry

4 tablespoons olive oil
2 large red onions, finely sliced
2 garlic cloves, finely chopped
2 tablespoons grated fresh ginger
1 teaspoon turmeric
3 Roma (plum) tomatoes, roughly chopped
2 red capsicums (peppers), cut into 2 cm (3/4 in) squares
10 curry leaves
400 ml (14 fl oz) coconut milk
3 x 200 g (7 oz) chicken breast fillets, cut into thick strips
3 limes, juiced
80 g (1 bunch) coriander (cilantro), roughly chopped
steamed white rice

Heat the oil in a large saucepan over a medium heat and add the onions and garlic. Cook for 3 minutes then add the ginger and turmeric. Cook for a further minute before adding the tomatoes, capsicums, curry leaves, coconut milk and chicken pieces. Simmer for 30 minutes then season according to taste. When ready to serve, add the lime juice and coriander. Serve with steamed white rice. Serves 4

buckwheat noodles with ginger broth

crab and watercress salad

100 ml (3 1/2 fl oz) tamarind water
2 tablespoons shaved palm sugar or brown sugar
2 tablespoons fish sauce
2 tablespoons lime juice
250 g (9 oz) fresh cooked crab meat
2 tablespoons light olive oil
2 tablespoons finely chopped coriander (cilantro) leaves
400 g (1 bunch) watercress, leaves picked
1 yellow capsicum (pepper), finely julienned
3 large red chillies, seeded and finely sliced
2 spring onions (scallions), finely sliced

To make the dressing, put the tamarind water, palm sugar, fish sauce and lime juice into a small bowl and stir until the sugar has dissolved. Set aside.

Put the crab meat into another bowl and break up the meat into fine threads. Add the olive oil and coriander and stir until well combined. Season with sea salt and freshly ground black pepper. Mix the watercress, capsicum, chillies and spring onions in a large bowl. Drizzle with the dressing and toss until all the ingredients are well coated. Divide between four plates and top with a large spoonful of the crab meat. Serves 4 as a starter

buckwheat noodles with ginger broth

400 g (14 oz) buckwheat noodles
1 litre (4 cups) chicken stock
1 tablespoon finely grated fresh ginger
2 teaspoons soy sauce
1 teaspoon fish sauce
3 spring onions (scallions), finely sliced
300 g (10 1/2 oz) fresh soft tofu, cubed

Cook the noodles until *al dente* and set aside. Put the stock, ginger, soy sauce and fish sauce into a saucepan and bring to the boil. Reduce the heat to low and allow to simmer for 5 minutes. Divide the noodles between four bowls and top with the spring onion and tofu. Ladle the hot broth over the noodles and serve immediately. Serves 4

potato, capsicum and zucchini curry

500 g (1 lb 2 oz) new potatoes, sliced in half
3 tablespoons olive oil
2 large red onions, halved and then sliced into eighths
2 garlic cloves, crushed
1 teaspoon turmeric powder
1 tablespoon grated fresh ginger
1 teaspoon fennel seeds, lightly crushed
3 red chillies, seeded and finely chopped
400 ml (14 fl oz) coconut milk
1 red capsicum (pepper), cut into thick strips
5 makrut (kaffir lime) leaves
500 g (1 lb 2 oz) small zucchini (courgettes), sliced
4 tablespoons lime juice
2 teaspoons fish sauce
3 handfuls coriander (cilantro) leaves

Put the potatoes in a saucepan and cover with cold water. Bring to the boil, cover and remove from the heat. Meanwhile, heat the olive oil in a saucepan over a medium heat and add the onions, garlic, turmeric, ginger, fennel seeds and chillies. Cook until the onions are soft then add the coconut milk, capsicum and makrut leaves. Add the strained potatoes, cover and simmer for 15 minutes. Add the zucchini and cook for a further 5 minutes. When ready to serve, add the lime juice and fish sauce. Garnish with coriander leaves. Serves 4

fresh and fast

- Fry some ginger and garlic in a wok with a little sesame oil and then add a bunch of roughly chopped watercress. Stir-fry until the watercress is just wilted then add a little soy sauce and lime juice. Serve with pan-fried whiting fillets or grilled chicken.
- Toss cooked buckwheat noodles in a little oil and flavour with cracked black pepper, pickled ginger, finely chopped chives and a little chilli. Serve with strips of lightly seared tuna or salmon.
- Grind 1 teaspoon of fennel seeds in a mortar and pestle and blend with a little mayonnaise, lemon juice and finely chopped dill. Serve with a salad of watercress and smoked salmon.
- Sauté sliced zucchini (courgettes) with a little garlic and olive oil. Season with sea salt and freshly ground black pepper and spoon into an ovenproof baking dish. Cover with finely grated Parmesan cheese and a sprinkle of paprika and grill (broil) until lightly golden. Serve as a side dish.

potato, capsicum and zucchini curry

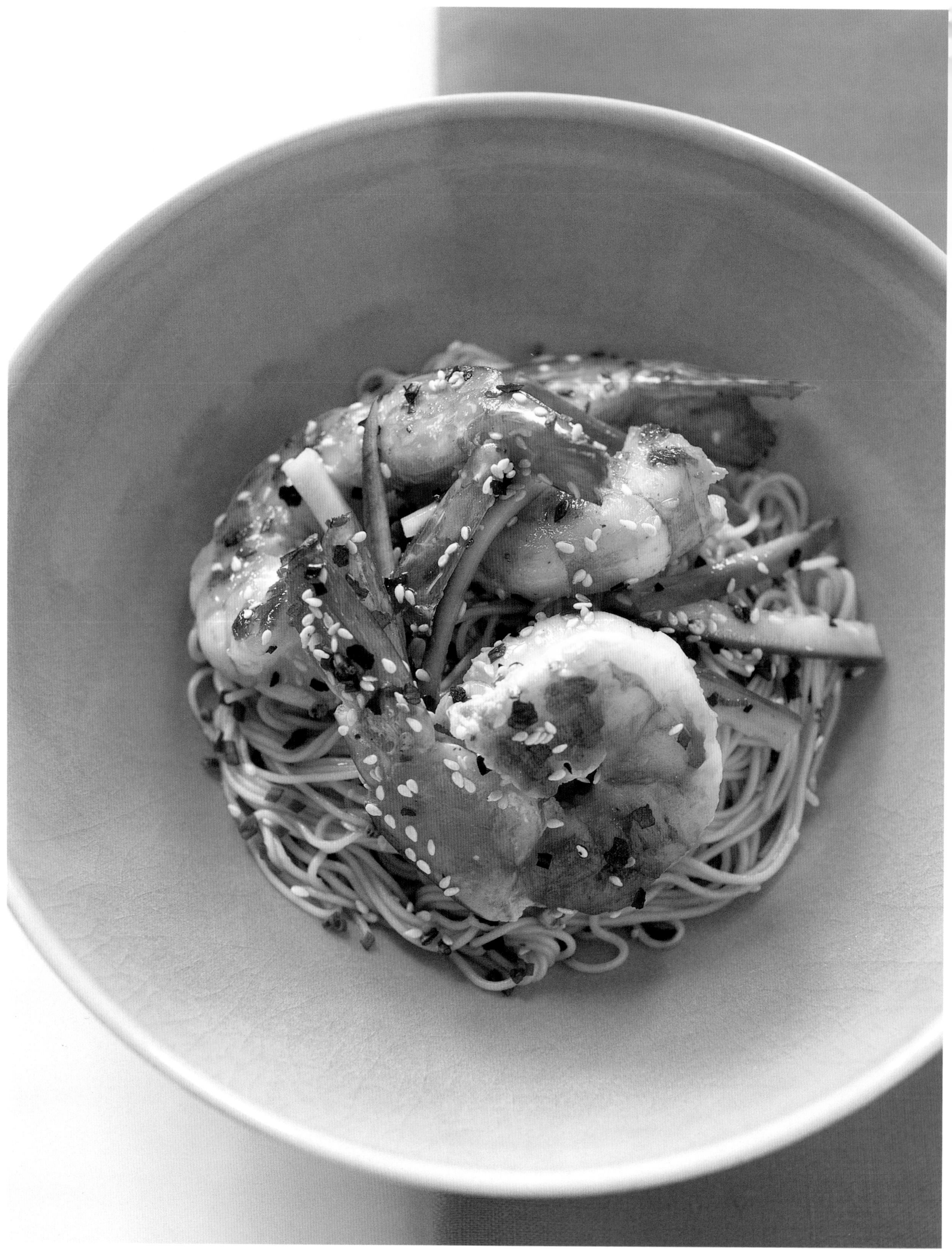

somen noodles with seared prawns

Finely slice ginger and marinate in Shaoxing rice wine and a little sugar for a light accompaniment to Asian-style dishes.

somen noodles with seared prawns

3 tablespoons rice vinegar
1 teaspoon finely grated fresh ginger
60 ml (1/4 cup) sweet mirin
1 tablespoon tamari
150 g (5 1/2 oz) somen noodles
1 tablespoon olive oil
16 large raw prawns (shrimp), peeled and deveined with tails intact
2 Lebanese (short) cucumbers, finely julienned
30 g (1 bunch) chives, finely chopped
2 tablespoons raw sesame seeds
1 teaspoon red chilli flakes

Put the rice vinegar, ginger, mirin and tamari into a small bowl and stir to combine. Set aside. Cook the noodles until they are *al dente*. Rinse the noodles and set aside. Heat a non-stick frying pan over a high heat and add the olive oil. Sear the prawns on both sides for approximately 2 to 3 minutes, or until they are pink and beginning to curl up. Put the noodles into a bowl with the dressing, cucumber and chives. Stir to combine then divide between four bowls. Top with the seared prawns. Put the sesame seeds and chilli flakes into a shallow saucepan over a medium heat and cook, stirring lightly, until the seeds begin to turn golden brown. Spoon the warm seeds over the top of the prawns and drizzle with any remaining dressing. Serves 4 as a starter

chilli tomato blue-eye cod

4 tablespoons olive oil
4 green chillies, seeded and finely chopped
1 teaspoon paprika
1 tablespoon finely grated ginger
1 red onion, finely sliced
1 tablespoon brown sugar
250 g (1 punnet) cherry tomatoes
4 x 200 g (7 oz) blue-eye cod fillets
10 thyme sprigs
2 tablespoons butter
1 handful coriander (cilantro) leaves

Heat the olive oil in a deep heavy-based frying pan over a medium heat and add the green chillies, paprika, ginger and red onion. Cook for 5 minutes then add the brown sugar, 200 ml (7 fl oz) of water and the cherry tomatoes. Continue to cook for a further 5 minutes and then add the fish fillets and cover with the thyme sprigs. Simmer for 5 minutes, or until the fish is cooked through. Remove the fish fillets and place on four warmed serving plates. Add the butter to the sauce and stir until it has melted into the tomatoes. Spoon the tomato sauce over the fish and garnish with coriander leaves. Serve with steamed green beans. Serves 4

fettuccine with chilli, corn and prawns

fettuccine with chilli, corn and prawns

2 tablespoons olive oil
2 small red chillies, seeded and finely chopped
1 teaspoon smoky paprika
3 spring onions (scallions), finely sliced
3 corn cobs, kernels removed
3 vine-ripened tomatoes, finely chopped
20 medium raw prawns (shrimp), peeled and deveined
with tails intact
400 g (14 oz) fettuccine
2 handfuls baby rocket (arugula) leaves
2 tablespoons extra virgin olive oil

Bring a large pot of salted water to the boil. Heat the olive oil in a large frying pan over a medium heat and add the chillies, paprika and spring onions. Stir-fry for 1 minute, then add the corn and tomatoes. Cook for a couple of minutes, or until the corn is soft and a deep golden colour. Add the prawns and continue to cook for approximately 2 to 3 minutes, or until the prawns are pink and curled up. Remove from the heat and season to taste with sea salt and freshly ground black pepper.

Add the fettuccine to the boiling water and cook until *al dente*. Drain and return to the hot pot. Pour in the corn sauce, add the rocket leaves and stir together. Divide between four bowls and drizzle with the extra virgin olive oil. Serves 4

chilli corn cakes

1 x 420 g (15 oz) tin creamed corn
125 g (1 cup) fine semolina
125 g (4 1/2 oz) mozzarella cheese, grated
125 g (4 1/2 oz) goat's cheese, crumbled
4 tablespoons finely chopped coriander (cilantro)
1 teaspoon baking powder
3 jalapeno chillies, finely chopped
2 eggs
6 bacon rashers
125 ml (1/2 cup) vegetable oil
4 handfuls baby English spinach leaves

Mix the creamed corn, semolina, mozzarella, goat's cheese, coriander, baking powder, chillies and eggs together. Season with sea salt and freshly ground black pepper.

Heat a lightly oiled non-stick frying pan over a medium heat and cook the bacon until crispy. Remove and keep warm until ready to serve. Add 2 tablespoons of vegetable oil to the pan. Add 2 heaped tablespoons of the batter to form a round corn cake and cook for 3 minutes on each side, or until golden and crusty. Remove and continue with the remaining batter, adding more oil when needed. Serve warm with the crispy bacon and baby English spinach leaves. Serves 4 to 6

lamb fillets with a sesame chutney

40 g (1/4 cup) sesame seeds, toasted
1 handful fresh coriander (cilantro) leaves
1 handful mint leaves
3 large green chillies, seeded and finely chopped
3 tablespoons tamarind concentrate
1 tablespoon shaved palm sugar
1 tablespoon olive oil
8 lamb loin fillets, trimmed (about 500 g/1lb 2 oz)
3 handfuls baby rocket (arugula) leaves

To make the sesame chutney, put the sesame seeds, coriander, mint, chillies, tamarind, palm sugar and 4 tablespoons of water into a food processor and blend into a smooth paste. Set aside in a small bowl.

Heat the olive oil in a large frying pan over a high heat. Add the lamb fillets and sear until blood begins to show on the uncooked side. Turn over and cook for a further minute. Remove from the heat and season with sea salt. Cover with foil and allow to rest for 1 minute. Slice the fillets and divide between four serving plates. Serve with a spoonful of the sesame chutney and rocket leaves. Serves 4

fresh and fast

- Pan-fry corn kernels with a little chilli, olive oil and some freshly chopped tomatoes. Season with sea salt and paprika before tossing with a bunch of roughly chopped coriander (cilantro). Serve as a warm salsa with chicken.
- Make a flavoured butter with fresh coriander, finely chopped black olives and a little ground cumin and paprika. Serve melted over hot corn on the cob.
- Serve the corn cakes with smoked salmon and a dollop of sour cream flavoured with horseradish for a brunch with a little bite.
- Finely chop a red onion and sauté in a frying pan with a little oil, some mustard seeds and turmeric. Remove from the heat when the onion is caramelized and sweet. Stir in some Greek-style yoghurt and finely chopped mint leaves. Serve with seared lamb.

lamb fillets with a sesame chutney

braised beef with shiitake mushrooms

Soak dried shiitake mushrooms and keep the richly flavoured soaking liquid for stocks and sauces.

braised beef with shiitake mushrooms

12 dried shiitake mushrooms
2 garlic cloves, peeled
2 star anise
1 large red chilli, seeded and roughly chopped
3 cm (1 1/4 in) piece fresh ginger, peeled and thickly sliced
1 daikon radish, peeled and cut into 1 cm (1/2 in) thick slices
2 carrots, peeled and sliced
4 x 150 g (5 1/2 oz) beef fillet pieces
3 tablespoons soy sauce
3 tablespoons mirin
6 spring onions (scallions), sliced into 2 cm (3/4 in) lengths
4 small zucchini (courgettes), cut diagonally into thick slices

Put the shiitake mushrooms into a large bowl and cover with 1 litre (4 cups) of hot water. Weight the mushrooms down with a small plate so they remain covered by the water rather than floating to the surface. Soak for 30 minutes before removing the mushrooms from the water and straining the liquid into a large saucepan or deep frying pan. Trim the mushrooms of any coarse stalks and put them in the saucepan with the garlic, star anise, chilli, ginger, daikon and carrot. Bring to the boil then reduce the heat to a simmer and cook for 10 minutes. Add the beef, soy sauce and mirin. Cover with a lid and continue to simmer slowly for a further 30 minutes. Add the spring onions and zucchini and cook for a further 5 minutes.

Serve with the vegetables spooned over the beef, surrounded by a pool of the cooking liquid, and a bowl of creamy mashed potato or steamed rice on the side. Serves 4

ginger spiced pork cutlets

1 teaspoon smoky paprika
1 teaspoon garam masala
1/2 teaspoon ground turmeric
1 tablespoon brown sugar
1 1/2 tablespoons grated fresh ginger
2 garlic cloves, minced
4 tablespoons olive oil
4 pork cutlets
lemon wedges
green salad
mashed potato (basics)

Put the paprika, garam masala, turmeric, brown sugar, ginger and garlic into a bowl. Stir in the olive oil to make a thick paste. Cover the pork cutlets with the paste and allow to marinate for 30 minutes. Heat a large non-stick frying pan over a high heat and sear the pork cutlets for 3 minutes. Turn the cutlets over, reduce the heat to low and cook for a further 7 to 10 minutes depending on their thickness. If the cutlets are particularly thick, cover the pan with a lid. Serve with a wedge of lemon, green salad and mashed potato. Serves 4

tofu salad with peanut dressing

braised eggplant with water chestnuts

tofu salad with peanut dressing

1 tablespoon shaved palm sugar
5 tablespoons boiling water
1 tablespoon balsamic vinegar
2 tablespoons kecap manis
1 red chilli, seeded and finely chopped
1 garlic clove, finely chopped
70 g (1/2 cup) roasted and ground peanuts
300 g (10 1/2 oz) hard tofu
90 g (1/2 cup) rice flour
300 ml (10 1/2 fl oz) peanut oil
60 g (2 cups) watercress sprigs
90 g (1 cup) bean sprouts

To make the peanut dressing, combine the palm sugar, boiling water, vinegar and kecap manis in a small bowl. Stir until the palm sugar has dissolved. Add the chilli, garlic and peanuts. Set aside.

Drain the tofu on paper towels and cut into small cubes. Put the rice flour into a plastic bag with a little sea salt and freshly ground black pepper. Add the tofu and toss until well coated. Heat a frying pan over a high heat and add the peanut oil. Deep-fry several tofu cubes at a time until they are golden brown, then remove with a slotted spoon and drain on paper towels. To assemble the salad, arrange the watercress and bean sprouts on four plates and top with the tofu. Drizzle with the dressing. Serves 4

summer salad with toasted pistachio dressing

2 Lebanese (short) cucumbers, finely sliced
90 g (1 cup) bean sprouts
1 red capsicum (pepper), julienned
1 orange, segments removed and finely sliced in half lengthways
30 g (1 bunch) chives, chopped into 2 cm (3/4 in) lengths
2 handfuls baby rocket (arugula) leaves
1 teaspoon finely grated fresh ginger
1 teaspoon honey
2 tablespoons lemon juice
1 teaspoon wasabi
4 tablespoons olive oil
130 g (1 cup) raw pistachios, toasted and roughly chopped

Put the cucumbers, bean sprouts, capsicum, orange, chives and rocket into a large serving bowl and toss to combine.

To make the toasted pistachio dressing, put the ginger, honey, lemon juice, wasabi and olive oil into a small bowl. Stir well to combine the ingredients and season with a little sea salt and cracked black pepper. Add the pistachios then pour over the salad. Serves 4 as a side dish

braised eggplant with water chestnuts

4 tablespoons olive oil
2 large red chillies, seeded and finely chopped
2 garlic cloves, minced
1 tablespoon finely grated fresh ginger
4 spring onions (scallions), trimmed and cut into 2 cm (3/4 in) lengths
2 eggplants (aubergines), cut into 2 cm (3/4 in) squares
225 g (8 oz) tinned water chestnuts, drained
500 ml (2 cups) vegetable stock (basics)
1 tablespoon soy sauce
1 tablespoon balsamic vinegar
150 g (5 1/2 oz) sugar snap peas
steamed white rice

Heat the olive oil in a wok or large frying pan over a high heat. Add the chilli, garlic and ginger and stir-fry for 1 minute. Add the spring onions and eggplant and cook for a further 5 minutes, or until the eggplant is soft and golden brown. Add the water chestnuts, vegetable stock, soy sauce and balsamic vinegar and reduce the heat to a simmer. Simmer until the liquid is halved, approximately 15 minutes. Meanwhile, blanch the sugar snap peas in boiling water until bright green. Drain and rinse under running cold water. Add the peas to the braised eggplant and cook for a further minute. Serve with steamed white rice. Serves 4

fresh and fast

- Make a salad of toasted pistachio nuts, couscous (basics) and coriander (cilantro) leaves and dress with chilli oil. Serve with grilled (broiled) chicken.
- Serve deep-fried tofu on a bed of stir-fried chilli, English spinach and finely sliced red capsicum (pepper), or as easy party food with a sweet chilli dipping sauce.
- Carefully add wasabi to crème fraîche to taste so that the cream has a light bite. Add finely chopped chives and serve as a small dollop on freshly shucked oysters or with lightly seared scallops.
- Heat 1 teaspoon each of finely chopped garlic and fresh ginger in a wok with some olive oil. Add cubes of eggplant and fry until the eggplant is cooked through. Splash with a little soy sauce and a scatter of finely sliced spring onions (scallions). Spoon over steamed silken tofu.

summer salad with toasted pistachio dressing

zesty

Oranges and lemons and the wonders of all things citrus. I doubt I could survive long in the kitchen without reaching for the humble lemon. There should always be a bowlful close at hand to add life to food or a twist of peel to a cold drink, and to bring sunshine into any room with the fruit's glowing colour. Whether it be a quick squeeze of juice over grilled fish or finely grated zest to revive a simple pasta, nothing really comes close to the lemon's unique tang. Its near relative, the orange, adds its own sweet zest to couscous and brings the taste of the aromatic Middle-East into wintry warm dishes. The cumquat, thought by many to be a purely ornamental tree, comes into its own baked with star anise and a plump free-range chicken while the grapefruit, often confined to the breakfast table, creates a sensation in a lunchtime salad. You don't need to look any further for fruitful inspiration.

fennel and grapefruit salad with rich apple dressing

jewelled couscous

fennel and grapefruit salad with rich apple dressing

500 ml (2 cups) apple juice
3 black peppercorns
2 thyme sprigs
1 tablespoon balsamic vinegar
1 teaspoon celery salt
2 fennel bulbs, very finely sliced
2 pink grapefruits, peeled and segments removed
2 celery sticks, finely sliced

To make the rich apple dressing, put the apple juice, peppercorns and thyme into a small saucepan and place over a medium heat. Bring to the boil and reduce until the liquid is syrupy and approximately 60 ml (1/4 cup). Set aside and allow to cool. Add the balsamic vinegar and celery salt to the cooled syrup and stir to combine.

Pile the fennel, grapefruit and celery on a serving platter and drizzle with the dressing. Serve with cold roast pork or chicken. Serves 4

jewelled couscous

15 saffron threads
1 tablespoon butter
185 g (1 cup) couscous
75 g (1/2 cup) currants
60 g (1/2 cup) slivered almonds, toasted
75 g (1/2 cup) raw pistachio kernels, toasted
1 orange, zested and juiced
2 tablespoons extra virgin olive oil

Put the saffron threads into a large saucepan with 125 ml (1/2 cup) water. Place over a medium heat and cook until the water has reduced by half. Add the butter and couscous and stir to combine. Add 250 ml (1 cup) of boiling water, cover and remove from the heat. After 5 minutes, uncover and fluff the couscous with a fork. Return the lid and allow to sit for a further 5 minutes. Put in a bowl and add the currants, almonds, pistachios and orange zest. Toss the ingredients together and then stir through the orange juice and olive oil. Season with sea salt and freshly ground black pepper. Serve as a side dish for roast chicken

marinated seared prawns with bruschetta

4 garlic cloves
1 tablespoon grated fresh ginger
1 large red chilli, seeded
1/2 teaspoon ground white pepper
1 tablespoon sesame oil
125 ml (1/2 cup) olive oil
1 lemon, juiced
16 large raw prawns (shrimps), peeled and deveined with tails intact
4 thin slices sourdough bread, cut on the diagonal
50 g (1 3/4 oz) baby English spinach leaves
2 spring onions (scallions), finely sliced

Put the garlic, ginger, chilli, white pepper, sesame oil, olive oil and lemon juice into a food processor and blend until combined. Put the prawns into a bowl, add the marinade and toss until they are well covered. Cover and place in the fridge for an hour. Toast the sourdough and put on separate serving plates. Pile with the spinach and spring onion. Sear the prawns in a frying pan over a high heat for approximately 2 to 3 minutes or until they are pink and beginning to curl. Divide the prawns between the four plates. Pour the remaining marinade into the pan and warm over a medium heat. Spoon the hot garlicky oil over the prawns and serve immediately. Serves 4 as a starter

fresh and fast

- Sear prawns (shrimps) over a hot grill (broiler) and toss them in olive oil, lime juice, a tablespoon of fermented Chinese black beans and roughly chopped flat-leaf (Italian) parsley leaves. Serve with somen noodles or steamed white rice.
- Make a quick salad of shredded Chinese duck, finely sliced grapefruit segments, watercress and sliced witlof leaves.
- Toss buttery couscous with parsley leaves, capers and finely chopped green olives. Serve with roast chicken or baked blue-eye cod fillets.
- Finely slice fennel and put into a baking dish with a little olive oil, lemon juice and finely chopped flat-leaf (Italian) parsley. Season, cover and bake in a 210° (415°F/Gas 6–7) oven for 30 minutes. Serve with pork sausages and mustard.

marinated seared prawns with bruschetta

lemon-braised vegetables

12 small kipfler potatoes
1 bunch baby carrots, trimmed of tops
6 sticks celery, chopped
6 tablespoons extra virgin olive oil
2 lemons, juiced
1 teaspoon sea salt
2 tablespoons finely chopped garlic chives

Preheat the oven to 180°C (350°F/Gas 4). Scrub the potatoes and carrots and remove any blemishes. If the carrots are too large, cut them in half. Put them into a casserole dish with the celery, olive oil, lemon juice, sea salt and 125 ml (1/2 cup) of water. Cover and put in the oven for 2 hours. When cooked, scatter with the garlic chives. Serve with roast chicken or baked whole fish. Serves 4 to 6 as a side dish

puy lentil and spinach salad

200 g (1 cup) Puy lentils
1 teaspoon sea salt
2 oranges
1 tablespoon balsamic vinegar
4 tablespoons extra virgin olive oil
1 tablespoon Dijon mustard
100 g (3 1/2 oz) baby English spinach leaves
8 red radishes, washed and finely sliced

Put the lentils in a saucepan with 1 litre (4 cups) of water and the sea salt, bring to the boil, reduce the heat and simmer for 30 minutes. Put the juice and finely grated zest of 1 orange into a large bowl. Add the vinegar, olive oil and mustard and stir to combine. When the lentils are tender, drain them of any excess water and add to the bowl. Season to taste with sea salt and freshly ground black pepper. Slice the skin from the remaining orange and cut away the segments. Arrange the spinach leaves, radish and orange segments in a serving bowl and then spoon over the lentils. Serves 4 as a side dish.

sesame chicken with coconut sauce

3 x 200 g (7 oz) chicken breast fillets, trimmed
1 tablespoon sesame oil
1 tablespoon light olive oil
1 tablespoon lemon juice
1 tablespoon sesame seeds
1 teaspoon sambal oelek or red chilli sauce
3 spring onions (scallions), finely chopped
200 ml (7 fl oz) coconut cream
125 ml (1/2 cup) tamarind water
steamed white rice
120 g (1 bunch) Asian basil
lime wedges

Slice the chicken across the grain into thin slices. Put them in a bowl and add the sesame oil, olive oil, lemon juice and sesame seeds. Stir until all the chicken is well coated in the marinade. Cover with plastic wrap and refrigerate until ready to use.

Simmer the sambal oelek, spring onion, coconut cream and tamarind water in a small saucepan over a low heat. Put a wok or large frying pan over a high heat. Add the chicken and stir-fry until cooked through. Arrange the chicken on a bed of steamed rice and spoon over the coconut sauce. Garnish with several sprigs of Asian basil and fresh lime. Serves 4

orange salad

3 leeks, trimmed
2 tablespoons olive oil
3 teaspoons soy sauce
3 oranges, peeled and finely sliced into rings
400 g (1 bunch) watercress
2 tablespoons extra virgin olive oil

Slice the leeks in half lengthways then rinse well in a large bowl of cold water. Cut the leeks into 3 cm (1 1/4 in) lengths and finely slice. Put into a large saucepan with the olive oil over a medium heat. Cover and simmer for 10 minutes or until the leeks are soft. Drizzle with the soy sauce, remove and allow to cool. Layer the orange slices with the watercress and leeks. Drizzle with a little olive oil and season with freshly ground black pepper. Serves 4 as a side dish

polenta pancakes with spinach and smoked salmon

warm vegetables with white beans

polenta pancakes with spinach and smoked salmon

250 ml (1 cup) milk
2 lemons, juiced
1 egg, lightly beaten
90 g (3/4 cup) self-raising flour
75 g (1/2 cup) polenta
1/2 teaspoon baking powder
1/2 teaspoon salt
50 g (1 3/4 oz) unsalted butter
1 tablespoon olive oil
2 handfuls baby English spinach leaves
12 smoked salmon slices
1 tablespoon salted baby capers

Combine the milk and half the lemon juice in a small bowl. Stir in the egg. Combine the flour, polenta, baking powder and salt in a large bowl. Add the egg mixture and whisk until a thick batter forms then stand for 30 minutes. Meanwhile, heat the remaining lemon juice in a saucepan over a medium heat and whisk in the butter. Remove from the heat when the butter has dissolved.

Heat a non-stick frying pan over a medium heat and add the olive oil. Spoon 3 tablespoons of batter into the pan for each pancake. Cook until the underside is golden brown then flip and cook for another minute. Repeat with the remaining batter. Top with the spinach, smoked salmon, capers and lemon sauce. Serves 4

chicken and pink grapefruit salad

1 spring onion (scallion), finely sliced
2 tablespoons white wine vinegar
4 tablespoons extra virgin olive oil
4 tablespoons crème fraîche
175 g (1 cup) roast chicken meat, shredded
2 pink grapefruits
3 handfuls mixed mizuna, lambs lettuce and English spinach leaves
8 walnuts, finely chopped

Put the sliced spring onion, vinegar, olive oil and crème fraîche in a bowl and stir to combine. If too thick, add a little warm water. Add the shredded chicken meat and toss so as to coat the chicken pieces all over. Using a sharp knife, peel the grapefruit and remove the segments by slicing between each of the membranes. Arrange a bed of mixed salad leaves on the serving plate and top with the chicken. Scatter the grapefruit segments and walnuts over the top of the salad and season with a little sea salt and freshly ground black pepper. Serves 4 as a starter

warm vegetables with white beans

6 tablespoons olive oil
6 slices pancetta, finely chopped
1 red onion, finely diced
2 garlic cloves, crushed
1 teaspoon finely chopped rosemary leaves
2 celery stalks, finely sliced
1 large eggplant, finely diced
2 red capsicums (peppers), finely diced
1 x 400 g (14 oz) tin chopped tomatoes
1 orange, rind grated and juiced
1 x 400 g (14 oz) tin cannellini beans, drained and rinsed
2 tablespoons roughly chopped flat-leaf (Italian) parsley
2 tablespoons extra virgin olive oil
crusty bread

Heat the oil in a large frying pan over a medium heat and add the pancetta, onion, garlic and rosemary. Cook until the onion is beginning to soften and then add the celery, eggplant and capsicums. When the eggplant is beginning to soften add the chopped tomatoes, orange rind and orange juice. Cover and continue to cook over a low heat for 30 minutes. Add the white beans and cook for a further 1 to 2 minutes then fold in the parsley and spoon into a serving dish. Drizzle with the extra virgin olive oil and serve with warm crusty bread as an easy meal or as a side dish to roast lamb. Serves 4

fresh and fast

- Bake 2 eggplants in a 215°C (415°F/Gas 6–7) oven until the flesh is soft. Scoop out the flesh and roughly chop into large pieces. Toss with a little tahini, lemon juice, flat-leaf (Italian) parsley leaves and season generously with ground cumin, sea salt and freshly ground black pepper. Serve with grilled (broiled) lamb cutlets.
- Slice the top off several red capsicums (peppers) and scoop out the seeds. Make a filling of steamed couscous, grated orange zest, finely sliced mint and some currants. Season with sea salt and freshly ground black pepper. Stuff the filling into the peppers and drizzle with olive oil. Return the tops and bake in the oven for an hour or until the peppers are soft. Serve with a salad of baby rocket (arugula) leaves.
- Finely chop dill and stir it into a small bowl of crème fraîche with lemon zest and freshly ground black pepper. Serve slices of smoked salmon on crisp toasts topped with the flavoured crème fraîche and a slither of dill pickle.

chicken and pink grapefruit salad

The aromatic cumquat lends a bitter sweetness to preserves and roast dishes.

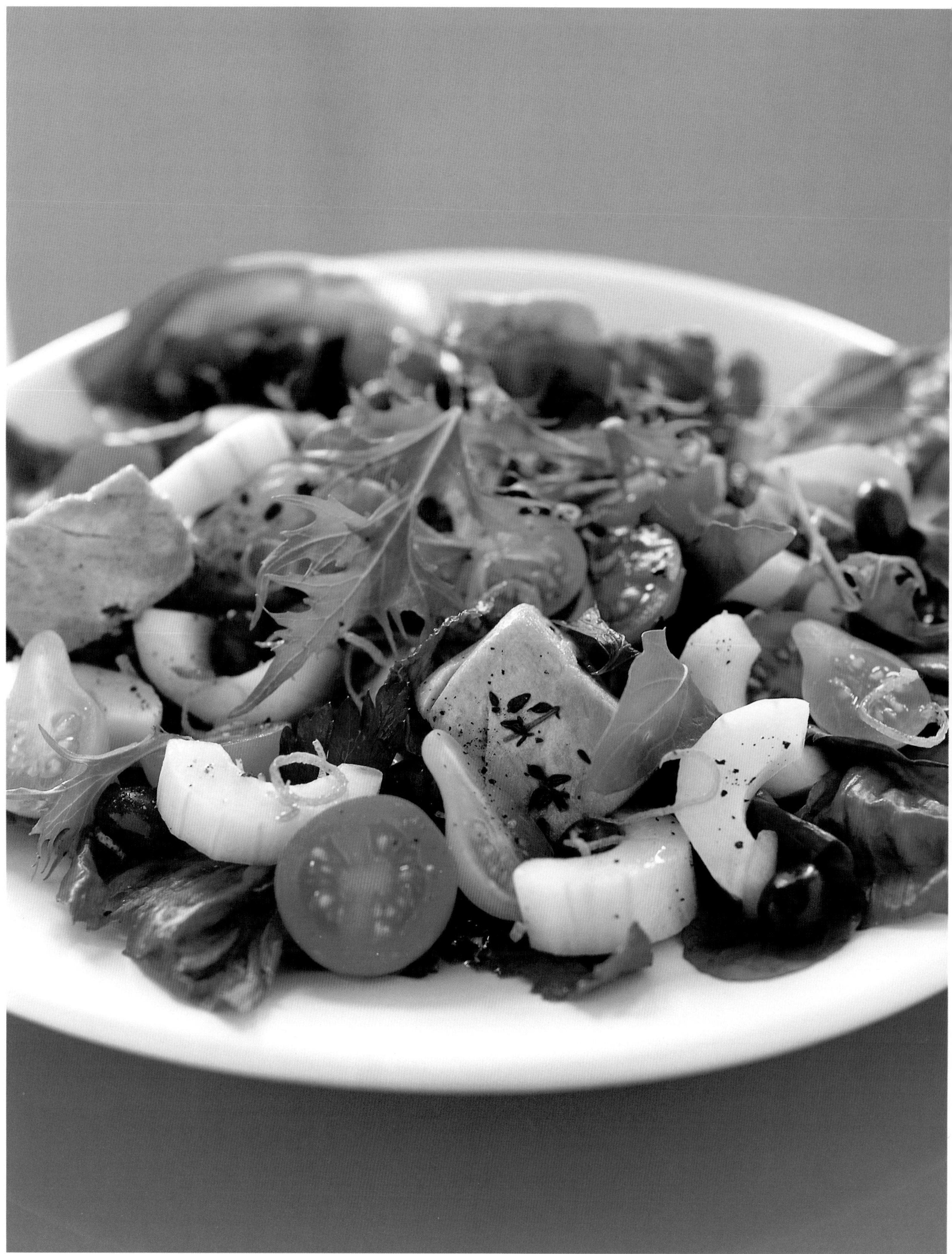

spiced cumquat chicken

1 x 1.8 kg (4 lb) organic chicken
16 fresh cumquats, halved
4 star anise
1 teaspoon Sichuan peppercorns
60 ml (1/4 cup) dessert wine, optional
2 tablespoons tamari or light soy sauce

Preheat the oven to 200°C (400°F/Gas 6). Rinse the chicken and pat it dry with paper towels. Put the halved cumquats, star anise, peppercorns and dessert wine into a small bowl and toss to combine. Put the spiced cumquats into the cavity of the chicken. Using a skewer, secure the opening so that the cumquats remain within the chicken.

Rub the skin of the chicken with the tamari and bake in the oven for 1 hour 15 minutes or until it is cooked through. Take the chicken out and check that it is cooked by pulling a leg away from the body—the juices that run out should be clear and not pink.

Remove the chicken and allow it to rest for for 10 minutes before carving. Serve with a spoonful of the baked cumquats and side dishes of creamy mashed potatoes and steamed green beans. Serves 4

tuna salad with fried lemon rind

800 g (1 lb 12 oz) tuna steaks
5 tablespoons olive oil
1 tablespoon lemon juice
1 tablespoon lemon thyme leaves
2 handfuls baby rocket (arugula) leaves
2 handfuls radicchio leaves
2 handfuls mizuna leaves
250 g (1 punnet) cherry tomatoes
90 g (1/2 cup) small black olives
1 telegraph (long) cucumber, peeled and seeded
2 organic lemons
1 handful flat-leaf (Italian) parsley leaves
extra virgin olive oil
lemon wedges

Cut the tuna steaks into several large pieces and cover them with 3 tablespoons of the olive oil, lemon juice and thyme. Allow to marinate for several hours. Put the salad leaves, cherry tomatoes and olives onto a serving platter. Cut the cucumber into large bite-sized chunks and add to the salad.

Remove the zest from 2 lemons with a vegetable peeler and cut into thin strips. Heat the remaining olive oil in a small frying pan over a medium heat. Cook the rind for 3 minutes and remove as it begins to turn golden brown. Drain on paper towels.

Heat a non-stick pan or grill and sear the tuna for a minute on all sides. Arrange the tuna pieces over the salad and scatter with the fried lemon rind and parsley leaves. Drizzle with a little extra virgin olive oil and serve with wedges of fresh lemon. Serves 4

asparagus with lemon crumbs

2 slices wholemeal bread
1 garlic clove
1 teaspoon sea salt
1 teaspoon thyme leaves
1/2 teaspoon roughly chopped rosemary leaves
1 organic lemon, zested and juiced
1 tablespoon olive oil
465 g (3 bunches) asparagus, trimmed
50 g (1 3/4 oz) unsalted butter, chilled and cut into cubes
40 g (1 1/2 oz) Parmesan cheese, finely grated

Preheat the oven to 200°C (400°F/Gas 6). Remove the crusts and put the bread into a food processor with the garlic, sea salt, thyme, rosemary, lemon zest and olive oil. Process until breadcrumbs form. Scatter the crumbs on a shallow tray and bake in the oven until golden brown.

Blanch the asparagus until it is bright green then drain and refresh in cold water. Put the lemon juice into a small saucepan over a medium heat and whisk in the cold butter. Remove from the heat when the butter is melted.

Divide the asparagus between four small plates and sprinkle with the breadcrumbs and Parmesan. Drizzle with the warm lemon sauce and serve immediately. Serves 4 as a starter

lime marinated fish

2 makrut (kaffir lime) leaves, finely sliced
2 limes, juiced
1 red chilli, seeded and finely chopped
1 teaspoon fish sauce
2 tablespoons grated fresh ginger
60 ml (1/4 cup) olive oil
80 g (1 bunch) coriander (cilantro)
4 x 150 g (5 1/2 oz) blue-eye cod fillets
tomato rice (basics)

Put the lime leaves, lime juice, chilli, fish sauce, ginger and olive oil into a large bowl and stir to combine. Remove the stems and roots from the coriander and wash carefully. Finely chop and stir into the marinade. Add the fish and toss until well coated. Cover and leave in the fridge to marinate.

Heat a frying pan over a medium heat and add the fish fillets. Sear on one side for 3 minutes before turning the fillets over and cooking for a further 3 minutes or until they are cooked through.

Put a large spoonful of the tomato rice on each of the serving plates, garnish with coriander leaves and then top with the fish fillets. Serves 4

vine leaf chicken

250 g (1 punnet) cherry tomatoes
1 handful mint leaves
1 handful flat-leaf (Italian) parsley leaves
250 g (1 cup) firm ricotta cheese
1 egg
4 x 200 g (7 oz) chicken breast fillets
12 whole vine leaves in brine
250 ml (1 cup) white wine
1 lemon, juiced
2 handfuls mixed baby leaf salad
2 tablespoons extra virgin olive oil

Preheat the oven to 200°C (400°F/Gas 6). Purée the tomatoes, 8 mint leaves and parsley in a food processor. Stir through the ricotta cheese with the egg and set aside. Pound the chicken fillets until they are 1/2 cm (1/4 in) thick. Put the fillets onto three overlapping vine leaves and spread the ricotta cheese mixture over the surface of each one. Season with freshly ground black pepper and a little sea salt. Roll up and secure with a toothpick or skewer. Arrange the parcels in a baking dish. Pour over the white wine and lemon juice and cover with foil. Bake for 30 minutes. Remove and allow to cool.

Unwrap and lay a vine leaf on a serving plate and top with salad. Slice the chicken and arrange on top of the salad with the remaining mint leaves. Drizzle with the extra virgin olive oil. Serves 4

lemon curry scallops

1 teaspoon butter
2 shallots, peeled and finely diced
1 teaspoon green curry paste
1 tablespoon finely chopped lemon grass
150 ml (5 fl oz) coconut cream
1 lemon, juiced
16 scallops on the shell, cleaned
1 handful coriander (cilantro) leaves
lime wedges

Put the butter, shallots, curry paste and lemon grass into a small saucepan over a low to medium heat. Cook for 3 minutes. Add the coconut cream and simmer for 2 minutes before stirring in the lemon juice.

Place the scallops, still in their shells, under a grill (broiler) for 2 to 3 minutes. Spoon a little of the creamy sauce over each scallop. Serve with a scatter of coriander leaves and the lime wedges. Serves 2 as a starter

osso bucco

lemon pasta

3 tablespoons extra virgin olive oil
15 basil leaves, finely sliced
3 tablespoons roughly chopped flat-leaf (Italian) parsley
2 garlic cloves, minced
2 lemons, zested and juiced
500 g (1 lb 2 oz) casareccia
75 g (3/4 cup) finely grated Parmesan cheese

Bring a large pot of salted water to the boil. Put the olive oil, basil, parsley, garlic, lemon zest and juice into a bowl and stir to combine. Cook the casareccia until it is *al dente*. Drain the pasta and return it to the warm pot. Add the lemon and herb oil and stir the pasta until it is well coated. Then add the Parmesan and stir again. Season with sea salt and freshly ground black pepper. Serves 4

osso bucco

4 x 4 cm (1 1/2 in) thick slices of veal hind shank
4 tablespoons plain (all-purpose) flour
1 teaspoon sea salt
4 tablespoons olive oil
1 leek, washed and finely sliced
1 celery stalk, finely chopped
1 x 400 g (14 oz) tin chopped tomatoes
250 ml (1 cup) red wine
1 orange, zested and juiced
rocket salad
polenta (basics)

Put the veal shanks, flour and sea salt into a clean plastic bag and toss until each shank is lightly coated in the flour. Heat the olive oil in a large casserole dish over a medium heat and brown the shanks, two at a time, on all sides. Remove and set aside. Add the leeks and celery and cook until the leek is soft. Add the tomatoes and cook over a high heat for 5 minutes. Add the wine, orange zest and juice. Stir to combine, then add the shanks. Cover the casserole dish and reduce to a simmer. Cook for 1 1/2 hours and serve with a rocket salad and warm polenta. Serves 4

ocean trout in tomato and orange marinade

4 x 150 g (5 1/2 oz) ocean trout fillets, skinless and boned
2 tablespoons olive oil
1 handful flat-leaf (Italian) parsley leaves
1 lemon, zested and juiced
1 orange, zested and juiced
500 g (1 lb 2 oz) vine-ripened tomatoes, finely diced
15 g (1/4 cup) finely chopped spring onions (scallions)
1 tablespoon small salted capers

Slice the trout into 4 cm (1 1/2 in) wide slices. Heat half the oil in a large, heavy-based frying pan over a medium heat and sear the trout for a minute on all sides. Put on a serving dish and season with sea salt and freshly ground black pepper.

Scatter the parsley over the fish. Add the lemon juice, orange juice, zest, tomato, onion and capers to the pan and cook for a minute. Pour over the fish and drizzle with the remaining olive oil. Allow to sit for 1 hour.

Serve the trout fillets on a salad of spinach leaves with a spoonful of the marinade. Serves 4

fresh and fast

- Combine the grated zest of 2 oranges and 2 lemons in a small bowl. Add some finely chopped parsley and season with sea salt and freshly ground black pepper. Toss together and set aside. Sprinkle the citrus blend over baked salmon or blue-eye cod fillets and then pour over a little melted butter. Serve immediately.
- For extra rich polenta, stir through a little crumbled blue cheese or a generous handful of grated Parmesan cheese. Serve blue cheese polenta with grilled pancetta and steamed broccoli. Serve Parmesan polenta with slow roasted tomatoes and grilled sausages.
- If plain lemon pasta is a little too simple for your tastebuds, add some finely sliced smoked salmon and capers to the recipe. For a heartier version add blanched broccoli florets and tinned tuna.

ocean trout in tomato and orange marinade

aromatic

Coriander, with its lush frilly leaves and fresh aromatic flavour, brings the taste of the East to the table. Similar in appearance to parsley, coriander is a herb of an entirely different nature. Its flavour is often viewed as a little strange on first tasting, but once acquired it becomes as necessary as basil and parsley. This versatile plant is full of surprises. Toast and then grind its seed in a mortar and pestle to create a pungent spice adored in the Middle East or scatter handfuls of fresh leaves over simple salads. Cumin is a spice which brings a wonderful warm depth to many dishes. There's nothing more mouthwatering than when the earthy rich aroma of toasting seeds hits the air and alerts everyone that an exotic meal is on its way. If you are a fan, then it is essential to freshly toast and grind the seeds yourself. It is only then that cumin's truly wonderful flavour really comes to the fore.

summer salad with spiced goat's curd

wild rice kedgeree

190 g (1 cup) wild rice
400 g (13 oz) fresh salmon fillet
curry sauce (basics)
1 lemon, halved for squeezing
1 handful flat-leaf (Italian) parsley leaves
1 handful coriander (cilantro) leaves
2 vine-ripened tomatoes, cut into eighths
4 eggs, soft boiled, cut into quarters

Preheat the oven to 180°C (350°F/Gas 4). Wash the rice in cold water and put in a saucepan. Cover with 1.5 litres (6 cups) of water and a pinch of sea salt. Bring to the boil then simmer for about 25 minutes, drain, fluff with a fork and set to one side.

Slice the salmon into 4 pieces and put in a shallow pan or baking tray. Bake for 5 minutes. Meanwhile, make the curry sauce.

Remove the salmon and squeeze the lemon over the top before breaking up the salmon into pieces. To assemble, toss the rice with half the herbs and a little of the curry sauce and arrange on individual plates. Top with the tomatoes, egg quarters, salmon, remaining herbs and a drizzle of the sauce. Serves 4

summer salad with spiced goat's curd

100 g ($3^1/2$ oz) goat's curd or light goat's cheese
1 teaspoon ground cumin
100 g ($3^1/2$ oz) green beans, trimmed
4 Roma (plum) tomatoes
2 Lebanese (small) cucumbers
10 mint leaves
2 spring onions (scallions), finely sliced
1 handful flat-leaf (Italian) parsley
4 tablespoons extra virgin olive oil
1 tablespoon lemon juice

Put the goat's curd into a bowl with the cumin and a generous grind of black pepper. Stir the ingredients together to form a soft, thick cream. If you are using a goat's cheese or a heavy curd, you might like to add a little milk to the mixture to make it softer and easier to stir.

Blanch the green beans in boiling salted water. When they turn bright green, drain and rinse under running cold water. Cut the beans into thin diagonal strips and put in a large bowl. Thickly dice the tomatoes and cucumbers and add them to the beans. Season with sea salt then add the mint, spring onions, parsley, extra virgin olive oil and lemon juice. Toss together and divide between four plates. Top with a spoonful of the goat's curd. Serves 4 as a starter

warm banana chilli salad

8 banana chillies
4 tablespoons extra virgin olive oil
1 tablespoon balsamic vinegar
1 teaspoon ground cumin
400 g (14 oz) flat green beans
10 large black olives, pitted and roughly torn
10 basil leaves, torn

Preheat the oven to 180°C (350°F/Gas 4). Put the banana chillies on a baking tray and bake for 30 minutes, or until the skin begins to blister. To make the dressing, put the extra virgin olive oil, vinegar and cumin in a small bowl and stir to combine. Blanch the beans in boiling salted water for 2 minutes, or until they turn bright green. Drain and rinse under cold running water.

To serve, cross two of the baked chillies on a plate. Top with the beans, olives and basil and drizzle with the dressing. Serves 4

fresh and fast

- Combine 2 cups of cooked white rice with the kedgeree curry sauce and some finely chopped coriander (cilantro) leaves. Stuff 8 red banana chillies with the flavoured rice and bake in a 210°C (415°F/Gas 6–7) oven for 30 minutes.
- Toss cooked wild rice with finely chopped roasted red capsicums (peppers), finely chopped red onion and fresh parsley leaves. Season and dress with extra virgin olive oil and a dash of pomegranate molasses. Serve with spicy grilled (broiled) sausages.
- Grill (broil) several banana chillies until the skin is blackened. Finely slice then toss with grilled (broiled) baby octopus, basil leaves, baby rocket (arugula) leaves and roughly chopped vine-ripened tomatoes. Season and drizzle with extra virgin olive oil.
- For a light and easy side dish, toss a selection of blanched green beans in extra virgin olive oil, lemon juice and fresh thyme leaves. Pile onto a serving plate and crumble some creamy feta cheese over the beans. Season with freshly ground black pepper.

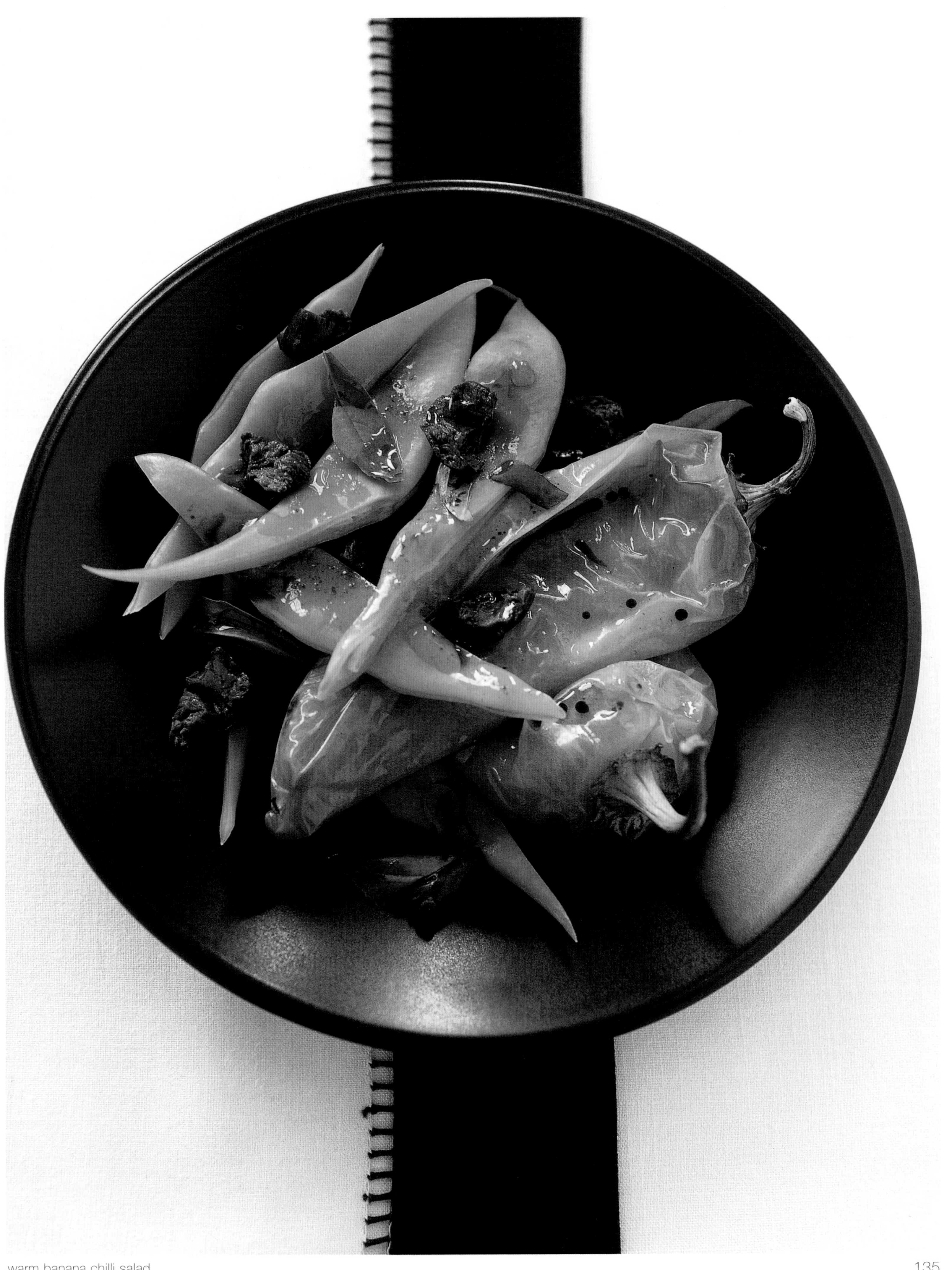

warm banana chilli salad

coconut greens

200 g (6 1/2 oz) French beans, trimmed
200 g (6 1/2 oz) sugar snap peas, trimmed
1 tablespoon olive oil
2 garlic cloves, minced
1 tablespoon very finely chopped lemon grass
1 teaspoon paprika
125 ml (1/2 cup) coconut milk
2 tablespoons fish sauce
1 teaspoon shaved palm sugar

Blanch the beans and peas in boiling salted water for 2 minutes, or until they turn bright green. Drain and rinse under running cold water. Set aside.

In a wok or large frying pan, heat the olive oil over a medium to high heat and add the garlic, lemon grass and paprika. Stir-fry for 1 minute before adding the coconut milk, 125 ml (1/2 cup) water, fish sauce and palm sugar. Reduce the heat and simmer for 5 minutes, stirring to make sure the sugar dissolves. Add the beans and peas and cook for a further minute. Spoon into a serving bowl. Serve with steamed rice and grilled (broiled) chicken or fish. Serves 4 as a side dish

grilled chicken with aioli

4 chicken maryland pieces
1 tablespoon finely chopped fresh thyme leaves
2 tablespoons ground cumin
1 teaspoon ground coriander
1 teaspoon paprika
1 lemon, juiced
4 tablespoons olive oil
green salad
aioli (basics)

Put the chicken pieces into a large bowl and add the thyme, cumin, coriander, paprika and 1 teaspoon of sea salt. Rub the spices into the skin and then drizzle the lemon juice and olive oil over the chicken. Cover and marinate in the fridge for a few hours or overnight. Preheat the oven to 220°C (425°F/Gas 7). Heat a barbecue and grill the chicken for 2 to 3 minutes on each side. Transfer to a baking dish and bake in the oven for 35 minutes. Check that the chicken is cooked through then serve with a green salad and a big dollop of aioli. Serves 4

chermoula kingfish

1 tablespoon cumin seeds, roasted
1 tablespoon coriander (cilantro) seeds, roasted
1 tablespoon paprika
1 tablespoon freshly grated ginger
2 garlic cloves
1 roasted red pepper (capsicum), seeded and skin removed
4 tablespoons roughly chopped coriander (cilantro) leaves
2 tablespoons olive oil
4 x 200 g (6 1/2 oz) kingfish fillets (blue-eye cod or a similar meaty fish can also be used)
lime wedges
creamy mashed potato (basics)

Preheat the oven to 200°C (400°F/Gas 6). Put all the ingredients except the fish, lime wedges and mashed potato in a food processor, or use a mortar and pestle, and process to a thick paste.

Rub the paste over the fish fillets. Put the fish, skin side up, on a baking tray and season with sea salt. Bake for 12 minutes. Remove from the oven and check that the fish is cooked through with the point of a small knife. Serve with lime wedges and creamy mashed potato or green salad. Serves 4

spinach and ricotta cheese omelette

4 tablespoons butter
1 onion, finely sliced
1/2 teaspoon cumin
pinch of nutmeg
500 g (1 bunch) English spinach, washed and trimmed
6 eggs, separated
4 tablespoons roughly chopped flat-leaf (Italian) parsley leaves
2 tablespoons finely chopped dill
200 g (6 1/2 oz) ricotta cheese
3 tablespoons grated Parmesan cheese

Heat a large heavy-based frying pan over a medium heat and add 1 tablespoon of butter, the onion, cumin and nutmeg. Cook until the onion is soft then add the spinach. Cover and steam for 2 minutes then remove from the heat and allow to cool. Beat the egg whites in a bowl until they form stiff peaks. Squeeze the spinach of any excess liquid and roughly chop. Combine the spinach and onion mixture in another bowl with the egg yolks, parsley, dill and ricotta. Season with sea salt and freshly ground black pepper then lightly fold in the egg whites.

Return the pan to a high heat and melt the remaining butter. Pour in the egg mixture then turn the down the heat to medium. Cook for 1 to 2 minutes. Sprinkle with Parmesan and place under a grill (broiler) until golden. Serve with wholemeal toast. Serves 4 to 6

red lentil soup

skewered swordfish with a spiced tahini sauce

red lentil soup

3 tablespoons olive oil
1 onion, finely diced
1 tablespoon grated fresh ginger
1 tablespoon ground cumin
2 carrots, peeled and grated
250 g (1 cup) red lentils
1 litre (4 cups) vegetable stock or water
2 red onions, finely sliced
80 g (1 bunch) coriander (cilantro), with roots attached

Put 1 tablespoon of olive oil into a large saucepan and add the onion, ginger and cumin. Cook over a medium heat until the onion is soft and transparent. Add the carrot, lentils and stock. Bring the soup to the boil then reduce to a simmer. Cook for 30 minutes, or until the lentils have completely disintegrated.

Meanwhile, heat the remaining olive oil in a frying pan over a medium heat and add the red onions. Thoroughly wash the coriander. Finely chop the roots and stems, leaving the top leafy section for garnishing later. Add the chopped coriander roots and stems to the red onion and continue to cook, stirring occasionally, until the onions are caramelized.

To serve, ladle the soup into four soup bowls, garnish with a generous sprinkling of coriander leaves then top with a spoonful of the caramelized onions. Serves 4 as a starter

spiced tomato and prawns

1 tablespoon light olive oil
1/2 teaspoon cumin seeds
2 large green chillies, seeded and finely chopped
1/2 teaspoon turmeric
250 g (1 punnet) cherry tomatoes, chopped in half
16 large raw prawns (shrimp), peeled and deveined with tails intact
125 ml (1/2 cup) coconut milk
1 handful Thai basil leaves
steamed white rice

Heat the olive oil in a frying pan over a high heat and add the cumin seeds, chillies and turmeric. Reduce the heat to medium after 1 minute, add the tomatoes, and cook for a further minute. Add the prawns and cook for 2 to 3 minutes on each side, or until they are pink on both sides and beginning to curl up. Remove the prawns and set aside. Add the coconut milk to the pan, season with sea salt and freshly ground black pepper and simmer for 1 minute. Meanwhile, arrange the prawns on four plates. Spoon over the coconut sauce and garnish with fresh Thai basil leaves. Serve with steamed white rice. Serves 4

skewered swordfish with a spiced tahini sauce

1 red onion
3 lemons
1 teaspoon caster (superfine) sugar
135 g (1/2 cup) tahini
2 tablespoons natural yoghurt
1 teaspoon ground cumin
4 swordfish steaks, cut into chunks
3 Lebanese (small) cucumbers, finely sliced on the diagonal

Soak four wooden skewers in water for 1 hour. Cut the onion in half and then finely slice into very fine strips. Put in a bowl and sprinkle with 1 tablespoon of sea salt. Leave for 20 minutes. Rinse the onion under cold water. Squeeze dry and return to the bowl with the juice of 1 lemon and the sugar. Toss to combine.

To make the spiced tahini sauce, combine the tahini iwith the juice of 1 lemon, yoghurt, cumin and 3 tablespoons of water in a bowl.

Slice the remaining lemon in half and then into thick slices. Thread the swordfish and lemon slices onto the skewers. Season with sea salt and set aside. Toss the cucumber and pickled onion together then divide between four plates. Heat a large non-stick frying pan over a medium to high heat and cook each fish skewer for 2 minutes on each side. Serve with the cucumber salad and tahini sauce. Serves 4

fresh and fast

- For a very quick and easy sauce, heat 400 g (14 oz) of tinned chopped tomatoes in a saucepan with 2 tablespoons of butter and 1 teaspoon of ground cumin. Simmer for a few minutes then serve with roast vegetables and lamb cutlets.
- Finely chop 3 vine-ripened tomatoes, 6 black olives, 2 anchovy fillets and some fresh basil leaves. Pour over extra virgin olive oil and allow to sit for 30 minutes so the flavours can combine. Spoon over grilled (broiled) swordfish and mashed potato.
- For a summery side dish, finely slice 1 red onion and sprinkle it with a tablespoon of white sugar and a little salt. Allow to sit for 30 minutes then cover with cider vinegar. Arrange thickly sliced ripe tomatoes on a serving platter and top with the drained onion. Drizzle with extra virgin olive oil and season with freshly ground black pepper.

spiced tomato and prawns

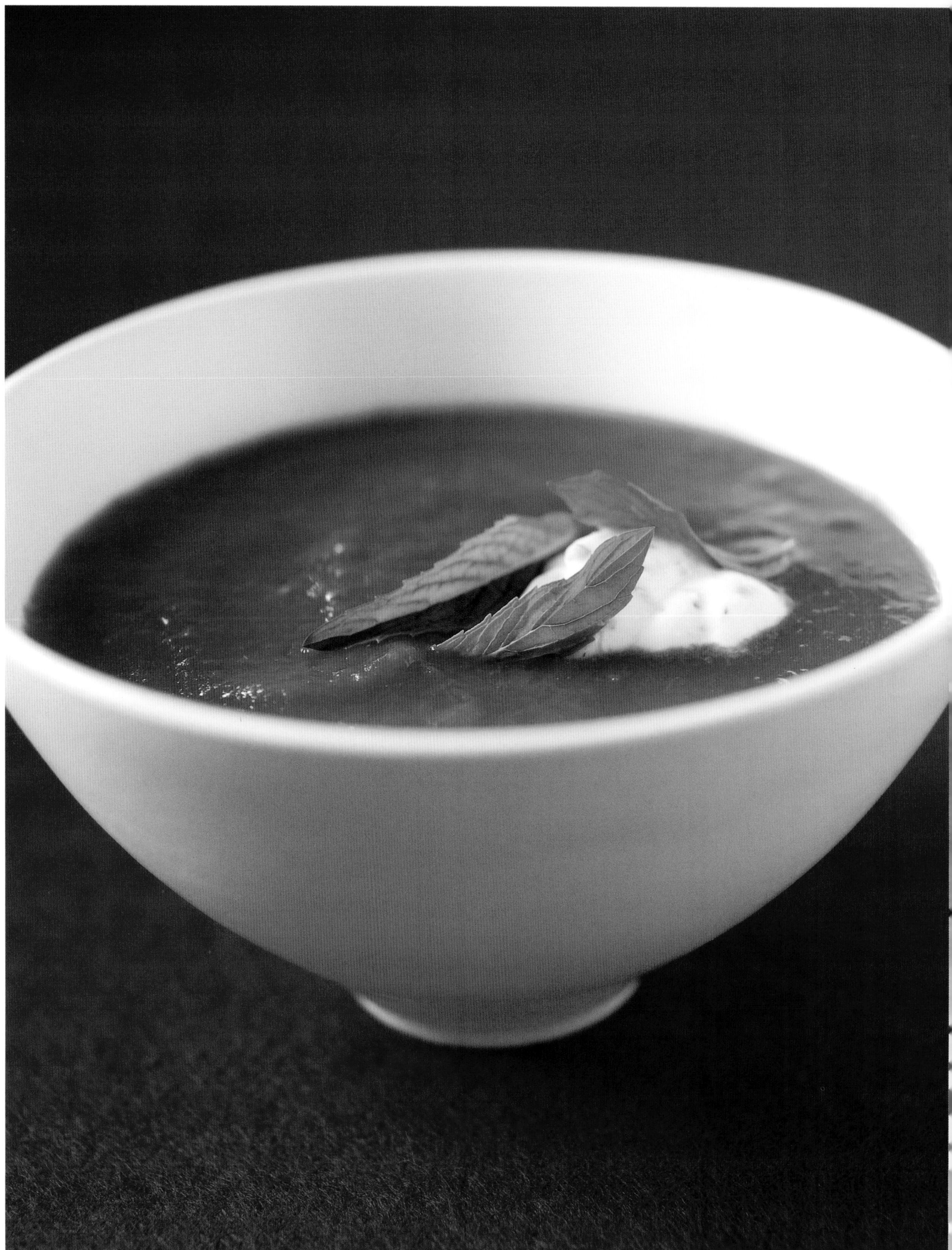

roast red capsicum soup with minted yoghurt

Roasting capsicums brings out the natural smoky sweetness of the flesh.

quince and red wine duc

roast red capsicum soup with minted yoghurt

4 red capsicums (peppers)
4 vine-ripened tomatoes, stems removed
1 tablespoon olive oil
750 ml (3 cups) vegetable stock
1 teaspoon finely chopped tinned chipotle chilli
1 teaspoon ground cumin
4 tablespoons natural yoghurt
1 tablespoon finely chopped fresh mint

Preheat the oven to 200°C (400°F/Gas 6). Put the capsicums and tomatoes into a baking tray and rub with a little olive oil. Bake in the oven for 30 minutes, or until both the capsicums and tomatoes are slightly blackened and blistered. Remove and allow to cool. Remove the skins and seeds from the capsicums and then put them into a food processor with the tomatoes. Process into a smooth purée and put in a saucepan with the stock, chilli and cumin. Bring to the boil and then reduce the heat to low. Simmer the soup for 10 minutes and season to taste with sea salt and freshly ground black pepper. In a small bowl, combine the yoghurt and mint. Ladle the soup into warmed bowls and add a spoonful of the yoghurt. Serves 4

quince and red wine duck

12 thyme sprigs
250 ml (1 cup) red wine
2 garlic cloves, sliced in half
4 duck breast fillets
3 tablespoons quince paste
1 teaspoon cumin
couscous (basics)

Preheat the oven to 200°C (400°F/Gas 6). Arrange the thyme sprigs over the base of a baking dish to form a bed for the duck. Add the wine and garlic to the dish. Rinse the duck fillets under running cold water and pat them dry with paper towels. With a sharp knife, make several incisions through the fatty skin on each of the fillets. Rub the quince paste into the skin, sprinkle with the cumin and season with sea salt and freshly ground black pepper. Sit the duck fillets on top of the thyme, flesh side down. Bake for 5 minutes then remove from the oven and spread the softened quince paste over the fillets with a knife. Return to the oven for a further 10 minutes. For crispy skin, put the cooked duck under a hot grill (broiler) for 2 minutes. Allow to sit for a few minutes then slice. Serve with couscous, a few thyme sprigs and a spoonful of the cooking liquid drizzled over. Serves 4

steamed eggplant salad

65 g (1/4 cup) tahini
60 g (1/4 cup) natural yoghurt
2 tablespoons lemon juice
2 teaspoons cumin
1 garlic clove, minced
2 eggplants (aubergines)
40 g (1/4 cup) toasted pine nuts
1 handful fresh coriander (cilantro) leaves
1–2 tablespoons extra virgin olive oil
1 teaspoon smoky paprika

To make the dressing, put the tahini, yoghurt, lemon juice, cumin and garlic into a bowl. Add 3 tablespoons of water and stir until smooth. Set aside.

Trim the ends off the eggplant. Thinly slice, widthways, and place into a steamer. Season with a little sea salt and freshly ground black pepper. Steam for 5 to 7 minutes, or until the eggplants are soft. Arrange on a serving plate, drizzle with the dressing and scatter with the pine nuts and coriander. Drizzle with the extra virgin olive oil and sprinkle with the paprika. Serves 4 as a side dish

rice with tomatoes and spinach

1 tablespoon butter
500 g (1 bunch) English spinach, washed and drained
400 g (2 cups) basmati rice
60 ml (1/4 cup) light olive oil
1/2 teaspoon ground turmeric
1 teaspoon ground cumin
1 red onion, finely sliced
2 vine-ripened tomatoes, finely chopped
750 ml (3 cups) vegetable stock

Melt the butter in a frying pan over a medium heat. Finely chop the spinach and add it to the hot butter. Cover and cook until the spinach is dark green and softly wilted. Remove and set aside. Wash the rice several times until the water runs clear.

In a large saucepan, heat the olive oil over a medium heat and add the turmeric, cumin and onion. Continue to cook for 5 to 7 minutes, or until the onion is golden and slightly caramelized. Add the rice and stir together for 1 minute. Squeeze any excess moisture from the spinach then add it to the rice along with the tomatoes and stock. Stir once then bring to the boil. Cover, turn down the heat to the lowest setting, and cook for 25 minutes.

Serve with yoghurt, grilled (broiled) fish and a wedge of fresh lime. Serves 6 as a side dish

spiced lentils with lamb cutlets

2 tablespoons olive oil
2 garlic cloves, crushed
1 red onion, finely diced
1 teaspoon finely chopped tinned chipotle chilli
1 teaspoon turmeric
95 g (1/2 cup) Puy lentils
1 x 400 g (14 oz) tin tomatoes, roughly chopped
12 small French-trimmed lamb cutlets
1 handful coriander (cilantro) leaves

Put the olive oil in a saucepan over a medium heat. Add the garlic, onion, chilli and turmeric and cook until the onion is soft and transparent. Add the lentils and cook for 1 minute, stirring the lentils into the onion mixture. Add the tomatoes and 500 ml (2 cups) of water. Cover with a lid and allow the lentils to simmer for 40 minutes. When the lentils are cooked, remove from the heat and season to taste.

Heat a non-stick pan over a high heat and sear the lamb cutlets on one side. Cook until the uncooked side begins to look a little bloody then turn the cutlets over and cook for a further 1 to 2 minutes. Season with sea salt and rest for a few minutes. Spoon the lentils onto four warmed plates. Top with the cutlets and garnish with coriander leaves. Serves 4

spiced ocean trout

2 tablespoons cumin seeds
1 tablespoon coriander seeds
2 tablespoons olive oil
2 leeks, washed and finely sliced
2 carrots, peeled and finely sliced
2 celery sticks, finely sliced
250 ml (1 cup) white wine
4 x 200 g (6 1/2 oz) ocean trout fillets
1 lemon, juiced
mashed potato (basics)

Put the cumin and coriander seeds into a large heavy-based frying pan over medium heat. Heat until the seeds begin to give off an aromatic smell. Remove from the pan and grind them in a blender, or a mortar and pestle, until they resemble a rough dust.

Return the spices to the pan and add the olive oil and leeks. Cook over a medium heat for 5 minutes. Add the carrot and celery and cook for a further few minutes, until both are beginning to soften. Add the white wine and 125 ml (1/2 cup) of water and place the trout fillets over this mixture. Season with sea salt and freshly ground black pepper and then cover the pan with a lid and reduce the heat to a simmer. Cook for 6 minutes. Remove from the heat and drizzle the lemon juice over the fish fillets. Serve with mashed potato and a spoonful of the spicy sauce. Serves 4

roast pumpkin and onions on couscous with harissa

salsa snapper

roast pumpkin and onions on couscous with harissa

800 g (1 lb 12 oz) pumpkin, cut into large bite-sized pieces
6 small spring onions (scallions), trimmed and halved
2 tablespoons extra virgin olive oil
185 g (1 cup) couscous
1 tablespoon butter
50 g (1 handful) baby English spinach leaves
harissa (basics)

Preheat the oven to 200°C (400°F/Gas 6). Put the pumpkin pieces and spring onions into a baking dish. Drizzle with extra virgin olive oil and season with sea salt and freshly ground black pepper. Bake for 20 minutes. Remove from the oven and turn the pumpkin and onions over. Return to the oven and bake for a further 20 minutes.

Cover the couscous with 375 ml (1 1/2 cups) of boiling water in a bowl and add the butter. Cover the bowl and allow to sit for 5 minutes. Fluff the couscous with a fork and then spoon onto four plates. Top with the spinach leaves, pumpkin and onions and then spoon over the harissa. Serves 4

salsa snapper

2 ripe tomatoes, finely chopped
1 Lebanese (small) cucumber, finely chopped
1/2 red onion, finely diced
2 large red chillies, seeded and finely sliced
1 handful coriander (cilantro) leaves
2 teaspoons ground cumin
2 teaspoons fish sauce
2 tablespoons lemon juice
4 tablespoons olive oil
4 x 200 g (7 oz) snapper fillets, skin on
2 tablespoons vegetable oil

Preheat the oven to 180°C (350°F/Gas 4). Lightly stir the tomato, cucumber, onion, chilli, coriander leaves, cumin, fish sauce, lemon juice and olive oil together in a small bowl. Season to taste with sea salt and freshly ground black pepper. Rinse the fish fillets and pat them dry with paper towels. Heat the vegetable oil in a large ovenproof frying pan over a high heat. Season the fillets liberally with sea salt and put them skin side down in the hot pan. Sear the fillets for 1 to 2 minutes until the skin is crisply golden and then turn them over.

Put the fillets in the pan in the oven and bake for 8 minutes, then transfer the fillets to a serving dish. Cover with a spoonful of the salsa and serve immediately. Serves 4

spiced pork with warm greens

2 tablespoons soy sauce
2 tablespoons mirin
1 tablespoon sesame oil
2 garlic cloves, minced
1 tablespoon brown sugar
1 teaspoon Chinese five-spice powder
4 star anise
1 tablespoon finely grated fresh ginger
2 small pork loin fillets (about 500 g/1 lb 2 oz)
1.4 kg (4 bunches) choy sum, washed
steamed rice

Put the soy sauce, mirin, sesame oil, garlic, brown sugar, Chinese five-spice powder, star anise and ginger in a large bowl and stir until the sugar has dissolved and the ingredients are well combined. Add the pork and marinate for at least 1 hour or cover and put in the fridge overnight. Preheat the oven to 180°C (350°F/Gas 4). Heat a non-stick frying pan over a high heat and add the pork. Sear on both sides until golden then transfer to a baking tray and bake for 10 minutes. Pour the remaining marinade into the frying pan with 125 ml (1/2 cup) of water and simmer for 3 minutes. Meanwhile, steam or stir-fry the choy sum until bright green. Remove the pork from the oven and allow it to rest for a few minutes.

Serve thin slices of pork with the warm greens, steamed rice and a spoonful of the sauce. Serves 4

fresh and fast

- Put bite-sized chunks of peeled pumpkin and sweet potato (kumara) into a bowl and drizzle with olive oil. Sprinkle with ground cumin, a little ground red chilli, sea salt and freshly ground black pepper. Roast in a 210°C (415°F/Gas 6–7) oven until golden brown and serve with grilled (broiled) sausages.
- Put a little brown sugar into a spice grinder with a star anise and grind. Rub into the scored fat of duck breast fillets and then bake. Serve with a salad of fresh orange slices and watercress.
- For an east–west twist on an old favourite, cook peeled and sliced green apples with 2 star anise. Sweeten with a little sugar and add a dash of balsamic vinegar. Serve with seared pork fillet or pork chops.
- Salsas are an easy and quick way to add flavour to fish or chicken. Combine finely chopped avocado, cucumber, chilli, coriander (cilantro) leaves and lemon juice; or green mango, red capsicum (pepper), spring onion (scallions) and lime juice. Season and spoon over the grilled (broiled) fish. Drizzle with olive oil and a scatter of fresh herbs.

spiced pork with warm greens

fragrant

One is the world's most expensive spice while the other is a common baking spice. Luckily for us a tiny pinch of saffron is enough to imbue any dish with its highly desired flavour. But without this culinary gold, centuries of cultural tradition would have to be rewritten. Imagine a bouillabaisse in Provence or a risotto in Milan without the benefit of those golden strands. Unlike these exotic hand-picked stigmas of the purple crocus flower, cinnamon, which is derived from the bark of the *Cinnamon verum* tree, has a far less exulted reputation. Most cooks around the world, regardless of nationality, are acquainted with the powers of this humble spice. Reminiscent to many of childhood rice puddings, discover its savoury side in African tagines and the rich meaty dishes of the Mediterranean. Cinnamon and saffron ... enjoy the fragrant combination.

chilli mussels

fish tagine

4 tablespoons olive oil
1 large red onion, roughly chopped
10 saffron threads
1 teaspoon ground cumin
4 large potatoes, sliced into bite-sized pieces
(about 750 g/1 lb 10 oz)
2 celery sticks, roughly chopped
1 x 400 g (14 oz) tin chopped tomatoes
1 small cinnamon quill
600 g (1 1/4 lb) thick snapper fillets, cut into 4 cm (1 1/2 in) chunks
1 handful flat-leaf (Italian) parsley leaves
2 tablespoons finely chopped preserved lemon

Heat the olive oil in a large deep-based frying pan or casserole pot over a medium heat. Add the onion, saffron and cumin and cook until the onion is soft and slightly caramelized. Add the potatoes, celery, tomatoes, cinnamon and 1 cup (250 ml) of water. Bring to the boil, then reduce the heat to a simmer and cook for 10 minutes. When the potatoes are soft, season the fish fillets with sea salt and add them to the stew. Simmer for a further 10 minutes then season with freshly ground black pepper. Garnish with the parsley leaves and preserved lemon and serve with warm crusty bread. Serves 4

chilli mussels

2 kg (4 lb 8 oz) black mussels
3 tablespoons olive oil
1 teaspoon red chilli flakes
3 garlic cloves, finely chopped
15 saffron threads
1 kg (2 lb 4 oz) tinned peeled tomatoes
3 tablespoons tomato paste
185 ml (3/4 cup) white wine
80 ml (1/3 cup) roughly chopped flat-leaf (Italian) parsley

Scrub the mussels and remove the beards. Rinse well in cold water and set aside. Heat the olive oil in a large saucepan over a medium heat and sauté the chilli, garlic and saffron for 1 minute. Add the tomatoes, breaking them up as you stir. Mix in the tomato paste and cook for 10 minutes. Bring to the boil and add the mussels. Cover and cook for 3 minutes, or until they have all opened, discarding any that haven't. Reduce the heat to a simmer and remove the mussels to four warmed bowls. Add the white wine and cook for another 2 minutes before ladling the hot soup over the mussels. Garnish with the parsley and serve with warm crusty bread. Serves 4

crab tartlets

250 g (1 punnet) cherry tomatoes
1 teaspoon chopped thyme
10 saffron threads
150 ml (5 fl oz) cream
2 egg yolks
2 tablespoons finely chopped chives
6 prebaked 8 cm (3 in) shortcrust tartlet shells (basics)
150 g (5 oz) crab meat
bitter leaf salad

Preheat the oven to 180°C (350°F/Gas 4). Put the cherry tomatoes and thyme in a small baking dish and bake for 20 minutes, or until the tomatoes are beginning to split. Meanwhile, heat the saffron threads with 80 ml (1/3 cup) of water in a small saucepan over a high heat until the liquid has reduced to 1 tablespoon. Put the saffron liquid in a bowl with the cream, egg yolks and chives then whisk together. Remove the cherry tomatoes from the oven and roughly chop, discarding any tough pieces of skin. Spoon the tomato mixture into the base of the tartlets and then divide the crab meat between them. Ladle the cream mixture into the tart cases and bake for 15 minutes, or until they are just set. Serve with a bitter leaf salad. Serves 6 as a starter

fresh and fast

- Steam open mussels in a little white wine flavoured with fresh thyme. Remove the mussels from their shells and marinate in olive oil, lemon juice, crushed garlic and finely chopped tomato. Serve with a salad of sliced waxy potatoes and baby English spinach leaves.
- For a quick but exotic pasta sauce, sauté finely chopped garlic and saffron threads in a little butter over a medium heat. Add diced fresh tomato and some tomato paste then simmer with a little water and a small cinnamon quill. Add fresh cooked crab meat to the tomato sauce and then fold the sauce through warm linguini. Garnish with coriander (cilantro) sprigs.
- Put bite-sized chunks of potato into a baking dish with whole cloves of garlic. Drizzle with olive oil and season with a little cinnamon and paprika. Rub the oil and spices over the potatoes and bake until golden and crunchy.

crab tartlets

chicken and miso soup

6 dried shiitake mushrooms
1 litre (4 cups) chicken stock
3 cm ($1^1/_4$ in) piece ginger, peeled and cut into thick rounds
1 small cinnamon quill
2 x 200 g (7 oz) chicken breast fillets, finely sliced on the diagonal
6 shallots, trimmed and cut into 2 cm ($^3/_4$ in) lengths
8 baby corn, cut in half lengthways
2 tablespoons white miso
100 g ($3^1/_2$ oz) sugar snap peas, trimmed

Put the mushrooms into a bowl and cover with 250 ml (1 cup) of hot water. Allow to soak for 10 minutes. Remove the mushrooms and strain the liquid into a large saucepan. Discard the tough stems of the mushroom and thinly slice the caps. Add them to the saucepan along with the stock, ginger and cinnamon. Bring to the boil then reduce to a simmer. Simmer for 10 minutes, remove the cinnamon and add the chicken, shallots and baby corn. Simmer for a further 5 minutes before adding the miso and peas. Heat the soup until nearly boiling and then ladle into four bowls. Serves 4

coconut spiced sweet potato

600 g ($1^1/_4$ lb) sweet potato (kumara), peeled and cut into bite-sized pieces
1 small cinnamon quill
2 large red chillies, seeded and finely sliced
finely grated zest of 1 orange
$^1/_2$ teaspoon ground nutmeg
1 x 400 ml (14 fl oz) tin coconut milk
80 g (1 bunch) coriander (cilantro)
$^1/_2$ teaspoon smoky paprika
couscous (basics)

Put the sweet potato, cinnamon, chillies, orange zest, nutmeg and coconut milk into a large saucepan with 250 ml (1 cup) of water. Bring to the boil and then reduce the heat to a simmer. Cook for 30 minutes, or until the sweet potato is soft and cooked through. Generously garnish with coriander sprigs and a sprinkle of smoky paprika. Serve on a bed of couscous. This side dish is wonderful served with chicken or pork. Serves 4

grilled chicken with almond salad

10 saffron threads
$^1/_2$ teaspoon ground cinnamon
1 teaspoon ground ginger
2 lemons, juiced
5 tablespoons olive oil
4 chicken maryland pieces
2 green capsicums (peppers), seeded and diced
45 g ($^1/_2$ cup) flaked almonds, toasted
1 handful flat-leaf (Italian) parsley leaves
1 tablespoon finely chopped preserved lemon
rocket (arugula) leaves

Cover the saffron with 3 tablespoons of boiling water in a small bowl. Leave to steep for 2 to 3 minutes. Meanwhile, put the cinnamon, ginger, lemon juice and 4 tablespoons of olive oil into a large bowl. Stir to combine the ingredients then add the chicken, saffron water and freshly ground black pepper. Cover and leave to marinate in the fridge for a few hours or overnight.

Preheat the oven to 200°C (400°F/Gas 6). Put the chicken into a baking tray, drizzle with the marinade then season with a little sea salt. Bake for 40 minutes. Meanwhile, heat the remaining olive oil in a frying pan over a medium heat. Cook the capsicum until it begins to soften then set aside. Add the almonds, parsley and preserved lemon to the capsicums and serve scattered over the baked chicken with a rocket salad. Serves 4

fish with a creamy saffron sauce

12 saffron threads
1 tablespoon olive oil
6 shallots, finely diced
1 large red chilli, seeded and finely chopped
1 teaspoon yellow mustard seeds
1 tomato, diced
1 teaspoon brown sugar
4 x 180 g (6 oz) perch fillets
4 handfuls baby English spinach leaves
185 ml ($^3/_4$ cup) coconut milk
lime halves

Cover the saffron with 250 ml (1 cup) of boiling water in a small bowl. Heat a large deep frying pan over a medium heat and add the olive oil and shallots. When the shallots are soft and transparent, add the chilli, mustard seeds, tomato, sugar and saffron water. Simmer for 3 minutes before adding the fish fillets. Cover and cook for 5 minutes.

Remove the fish to four warmed serving plates and pile the spinach leaves beside the fillets. Add the coconut milk to the sauce and simmer for 1 minute before spooning it over the fish. Serve with fresh lime and steamed white rice. Serves 4

parmesan lamb pies

2 tablespoons olive oil
2 onions, peeled and finely diced
2 garlic cloves, chopped
500 g (1 lb 2 oz) lamb mince
2 celery stalks, finely chopped
40 g (1/4 cup) grated carrot
1 teaspoon ground cinnamon
1 x 400 g (14 oz) tin chopped tomatoes
250 ml (1 cup) red wine
3 eggs
200 ml (7 fl oz) Greek-style yoghurt
100 g (3 1/2 oz) grated Parmesan cheese

Preheat the oven to 200°C (400°F/Gas 6). Heat the olive oil in a frying pan over a medium heat then add the onions and garlic. Cook until the onion is beginning to soften and turn a golden brown. Add the mince and turn up the heat. Brown the mince and add the celery, carrot, cinnamon, tomato and wine. Reduce the heat to medium and simmer until the liquid has reduced. Season to taste with freshly ground black pepper and sea salt. Spoon the mixture into four individual ramekins or a large baking dish. Put the eggs, yoghurt and half the Parmesan into a bowl and whisk to combine. Spoon the mixture over the pies and sprinkle with the remaining Parmesan. Bake for 20 minutes, or until the top is golden brown. Serves 4

moroccan lamb

125 ml (1/2 cup) lemon juice
3 tablespoons olive oil
1 teaspoon ground cinnamon
3 garlic cloves, sliced
1 teaspoon cumin
finely grated zest of 1 orange
2 lamb backstraps, trimmed (about 500 g/1 lb 2 oz)
1 handful flat-leaf (Italian) parsley leaves
20 mint leaves, roughly chopped
20 fresh oregano leaves
2 vine-ripened tomatoes, roughly chopped

Put the lemon juice, olive oil, cinnamon, garlic, cumin and orange zest in a glass or ceramic bowl and stir to combine. Add the lamb, cover and place in the fridge for 3 hours or overnight.

Remove the lamb from the marinade and sear in a non-stick frying pan over a high heat. Cook until the uncooked side is beginning to look a little bloody then turn the lamb over, reduce the heat and cook for a further 5 minutes. Allow the lamb to rest for a few minutes. Toss the fresh herbs and tomato together in a bowl and divide between four plates. Slice the lamb across the grain and arrange over the tomato salad. Serve with warm couscous. Serves 4

lemon and saffron risotto

1 litre (4 cups) vegetable stock (basics)
50 g (1 3/4 oz) butter
1 onion, finely diced
15 saffron threads
275 g (1 1/4 cups) risotto rice
155 g (1 bunch) asparagus
2 tablespoons lemon juice
80 g (2 3/4 oz) grated Parmesan cheese

Heat the stock in a large saucepan over a high heat. When it is almost boiling, reduce the heat to a simmer. Melt the butter in a large heavy-based saucepan over a medium heat. Add the onion and saffron and cook until the onion is soft and transparent. Add the rice and stir until the grains are glossy and well coated in the buttery saffron. Add 250 ml (1 cup) of hot stock and stir until it is absorbed. Continue to add the stock until it is all absorbed and the rice is tender. Bring a saucepan of water to the boil and quickly blanch the asparagus until it is bright green. Drain and slice into small pieces. Add the lemon juice and Parmesan to the risotto and season with sea salt and freshly ground black pepper. Spoon into warm bowls and top with asparagus spears. Serves 4

fresh and fast

- Finely dice ripe tomatoes and red onion and toss with fresh oregano. Season with sea salt and freshly ground black pepper. Drizzle with extra virgin olive oil and spoon onto toasted sourdough. Top with a spoonful of soft goat's curd and a sprinkle of paprika.
- Make a bed of English spinach leaves and top with blanched asparagus and finely chopped preserved lemon. Heat a few saffron threads with 4 tablespoons of butter until the butter begins to bubble and turn golden brown. Spoon the hot butter over the asparagus and serve.
- Finely slice several onions and sauté with a little ground cinnamon and olive oil. When the onion is caramelized, add a little finely chopped preserved lemon and flat-leaf (Italian) parsley. Serve with seared lamb fillets.
- Roughly chop tomatoes and simmer them with cinnamon and saffron. Add a few handfuls of baby English spinach leaves and continue to cook until the spinach has wilted. Season with salt and pepper and fold through steamed couscous.

moroccan lamb

The pungent curry leaf is most commonly used to flavour Indian curries.

blue-eye cod with saffron and capers

cashew curry

2 onions, diced
3 garlic cloves, crushed
4 cm (1 1/2 in) piece fresh ginger, chopped
1 tablespoon olive oil
1 teaspoon turmeric
1 small cinnamon quill
6 curry leaves
1 lime, juiced
3 red capsicums (peppers), cut into 1 cm (1/2 in) squares
250 g (9 oz) raw cashews
1 x 400 ml (14 fl oz) tin coconut milk
2 large red chillies, seeded and finely chopped
2 handfuls coriander (cilantro) leaves
steamed white rice

Put the onions, garlic and ginger into a food processor and process into a paste. Heat the olive oil in a heavy-based saucepan over a medium heat and add the onion paste. Cook for 5 minutes. Add the turmeric, cinnamon, curry leaves and lime juice and cook for 2 to 3 minutes. Add the capsicums and cashews. Stir then add the coconut milk and 250 ml (1 cup) of water. Simmer for 1 hour. Place the curry into a large serving bowl and top with the chillies and coriander leaves. Serve with steamed white rice. Serves 4

blue-eye cod with saffron and capers

4 Roma (plum) tomatoes, thickly diced
1 leek, washed and finely sliced
10 strands saffron
1 tablespoon salted capers
250 ml (1 cup) white wine
4 x 200 g (6 1/2 oz) blue-eye cod fillets
1 tablespoon butter
2 tablespoons small black olives
1 handful flat-leaf (Italian) parsley leaves
boiled potatoes

Preheat the oven to 180°C (350°F/Gas 4). Meanwhile, put the tomato in the bottom of a stoveproof casserole or baking dish over a medium heat. Top with the leek then sprinkle the saffron and capers over. Add the wine and bring to the boil. Reduce the heat to a simmer and cook for a further 10 minutes. Add the fish then season lightly with sea salt and freshly ground black pepper and dot with a little butter. Cover and bake in the oven for 15 minutes.

Remove and place the fish on warmed serving plates. Spoon over the sauce then garnish with the olives and parsley. Serve with boiled potatoes. Serves 4

roast vegetables with rouille

a selection of parsnips, onions, fennel, carrots, zucchini, pumpkin and sweet potato (kumara)
4 tablespoons olive oil
1 thick slice sourdough bread
10 saffron threads
1 red capsicum (pepper), roasted and skinned
1/4 teaspoon paprika
1 garlic clove
125 ml (1/2 cup) light olive oil

Preheat the oven to 200°C (400°F/Gas 6). Choose a selection of your favourite roasting vegetables and cut them into large chunks. Put into a baking dish and rub with the olive oil. Cover with foil and bake for 1 hour.

To make the rouille, tear the bread into pieces and put it in a bowl. Bring the saffron threads and 60 ml (1/4 cup) of water to the boil in a small saucepan and simmer for 1 minute. Soak the bread in the hot saffron water then add it to a food processor or blender with the capsicum, paprika and garlic. Blend to form a smooth paste, then add the light olive oil in a steady stream.

To serve, arrange the vegetables on a serving plate with the rouille. Serves 4

saffron squid and chive salad

300 g (10 1/2 oz) orecchiette
3 tablespoons lemon juice
7 tablespoons extra virgin olive oil
30 g (1 bunch) chives, chopped into 1 cm (1/2 in) lengths
2 small red chillies, seeded and finely chopped
2 tablespoons olive oil
10 saffron threads
1 large red onion, finely diced
6 small squid, cleaned
1 handful flat-leaf (Italian) parsley leaves, roughly chopped
2 handfuls baby rocket (arugula) leaves

Bring a large pot of salted water to the boil and cook the orecchiette until *al dente*. Drain and set aside. Meanwhile, put the lemon juice, extra virgin olive oil, chives and chillies into a large bowl and stir to combine. Heat a large non-stick frying pan over a medium heat and add the olive oil and saffron. After 1 minute add the onion and cook until it is soft and transparent. Remove most of the onion from the pan with a slotted spoon and add it to the dressing in the bowl.

Increase the heat and quickly sauté the squid — they should only need a few minutes on each side. Roughly slice the cooked squid and add to the dressing. Season with sea salt and freshly ground black pepper. Add the pasta and toss together. Pile into a large bowl with the parsley and rocket. Serves 4

baked leeks with seared salmon

3 leeks, washed
4 spring onions (scallions), trimmed
10 saffron threads
1 tablespoon salted capers
2 tablespoons butter
1 tablespoon olive oil
4 x 150 g (5 1/2 oz) salmon fillets
2 handfuls baby English spinach leaves

Preheat the oven to 180°C (350°F/Gas 4). Cut the leeks and spring onions into short lengths and put them in a baking dish with the saffron, capers, butter and 185 ml (3/4 cup) of water. Cover with foil and bake for 1 hour. Heat a non-stick pan over a high heat and add the olive oil. Sear the salmon, skin side down, for 2 minutes, then turn over. Cover, reduce the heat and cook for a further 3 minutes. Divide the spinach leaves between four plates. Top with the salmon and spoon over the baked leeks. Serves 4

leek, saffron and chickpea soup

2 tablespoons butter
15 saffron threads
3 leeks, cleaned and finely diced
1 lemon, zest peeled into thick strips
1 carrot, peeled and grated
3 tablespoons roughly chopped flat-leaf (Italian) parsley
1 litre (4 cups) chicken stock
1 x 400 g (14 oz) tin chickpeas, drained and rinsed

Heat the butter and saffron threads in a large saucepan over a medium heat. Add the leeks when the butter begins to bubble and cook until they are soft and transparent. Add the lemon zest, carrot and parsley and cook for a further minute before adding the stock and chickpeas. Bring to the boil then reduce the heat and simmer for 15 minutes. Serves 4

chilli mint lamb with saffron vegetables

seaside risoni

210 g (1 cup) risoni
2 tablespoons butter
12 saffron threads
2 garlic cloves, minced
1 x 400 g (14 oz) tin chopped tomatoes
500 ml (2 cups) white wine
12 large raw prawns (shrimp), peeled and deveined with tails intact
16 black mussels, cleaned
2 tablespoons finely chopped preserved lemon
1 handful flat-leaf (Italian) parsley leaves

Bring a large pot of salted water to the boil. Cook the risoni until it is *al dente* then drain and set aside. In a deep wide frying pan or wok, heat the butter, saffron and garlic until the butter begins to bubble. Add the tomatoes and white wine and simmer for 2 minutes. Add the risoni, prawns and mussels to the tomato mixture and cover the pan with a lid. Simmer until the mussels have opened, discarding any that don't. Remove from the heat and divide the mixture between four warm pasta bowls. Garnish with preserved lemon and parsley leaves. Serves 4

saffron mash with roast beets and mushrooms

8 baby beetroots
300 g (10 1/2 oz) mixed pine, oyster and fresh shiitake mushrooms
3 tablespoons extra virgin olive oil
2 garlic cloves, finely sliced
8 thyme sprigs
1 kg (2 lb 4 oz) desiree potatoes, peeled and cut into chunks
125 ml (1/2 cup) milk
15 saffron threads
100 g (3 1/2 oz) butter
4 tablespoons toasted pumpkin seeds (pepitas)

Preheat the oven to 200°C (400°F/Gas 6). Put the beetroots in a baking dish with 125 ml (1/2 cup) of water. Cover with foil and bake for 1 hour, or until cooked. Rub the skin off the cooked beetroots then slice in half and wrap in foil. Bake the mushrooms with olive oil, garlic and thyme in a baking dish covered with foil for 30 minutes. Return the mushrooms and beetroots just prior to serving to the oven to warm. Meanwhile, cook the potatoes in a pot of salted water. Heat the milk, saffron and butter in a saucepan over a medium to low heat until the saffron begins to colour the milk. Mash the potatoes while still warm then whisk in the saffron milk. Season with sea salt. Cut the warmed beetroot into quarters and serve with the mash and mushrooms. Sprinkle with toasted pumpkin seeds and thyme sprigs from the baking dish. Serves 4

chilli mint lamb with saffron vegetables

3 tablespoons olive oil
2 tablespoons harissa
80 g (1 bunch) mint, leaves removed and finely chopped
25 g (1/2 cup) coriander leaves, finely chopped
4 French-trimmed lamb racks
3 onions, peeled and quartered
3 parsnips, peeled and cut into chunks
4 waxy potatoes, peeled and cut into chunks
600 g (1 lb 5 oz) pumpkin, peeled and cut into chunks
1 teaspoon sugar
1/2 teaspoon crushed fennel seeds
20 black olives, pitted
1 teaspoon ground cumin
10 saffron threads
3 tablespoons lemon juice

Preheat the oven to 220°C (425°F/Gas 7). Mix 2 tablespoons of the olive oil, harissa and herbs in a bowl then rub into the lamb racks. Season with sea salt and freshly ground black pepper. Put the vegetables into a baking dish and toss with the remaining olive oil, sugar, fennel seeds, olives, cumin, saffron and lemon juice. Cover with foil and bake for 30 minutes, then turn the vegetables and return uncovered to the oven. Sear the lamb in a frying pan over a high heat then put on top of the vegetables. Bake for a further 20 minutes. Rest the lamb for 2 to 3 minutes, slice and serve with the vegetables. Serves 4

fresh and fast

- Sauté finely sliced spring onions (scallions) in butter with some saffron threads. Add peeled raw prawns (shrimp) and cook until the prawns are pink and curled. Remove the prawns with a slotted spoon and add a tin of crushed tomatoes. Season with sea salt and freshly ground black pepper then simmer for a few minutes. Return the prawns to the frying pan and serve with steamed rice.
- Quarter fresh shiitake mushrooms and sauté them with a little butter and finely sliced pancetta. Add a splash of red wine and serve with buttery couscous.
- Slice pumpkin into bite-sized pieces and season with sea salt, black pepper and a little ground cinnamon. Roast in a 210°C (415°F/Gas 6–7) oven until golden brown and then remove and allow to cool. Arrange the roast pumpkin on a serving plate with a mixed leaf salad and halved cherry tomatoes. Drizzle with a light sour cream and sprinkle with toasted pumpkin seeds (pepitas).

saffron mash with roast beets and mushrooms

ambrosial

Sugar and spice and all things nice, that's what the most heavenly desserts are made from. A plump fig marinated in sweet wine or the summery sweetness of ripe peaches infused with vanilla. Who could resist such easy temptations? And why stop there, be brave with the sweet side of spice and combine cumin with sugar and lime for a sweet Middle-Eastern twist on the simple cookie. Or allow the subtle perfume of rose-water to cut through the richness of a sublime chocolate marquise and transform a rice pudding from the everyday to the extraordinary with a scatter of fresh pistachios. Mix these flavours with the intoxicating scents of ebony black vanilla beans and aromatic cardamom and dessert will never be the same again. Ambrosial literally means food of the gods, and, with dishes like these, who can argue.

rose-tinged rice pudding

rhubarb fool

400 g (14 oz) rhubarb
2 tablespoons sugar
2 oranges, juiced
115 g (1/2 cup) dark brown sugar
300 ml (10 1/2 fl oz) cream, whipped

Trim and rinse the rhubarb before chopping it into 2 cm (3/4 in) lengths. Put the rhubarb into a saucepan over a low heat with the sugar and orange juice. Cover and simmer for 15 minutes. Remove and allow to cool. Spoon a little of the rhubarb into the base of four glass serving bowls. Sprinkle with brown sugar and top with the whipped cream. Spoon another layer of rhubarb over the cream and lightly sprinkle with more brown sugar. Serve with cardamom almond bread (basics). Serves 4

rose-tinged rice pudding

500 ml (2 cups) milk
55 g (1/4 cup) granulated sugar
2 teaspoons finely grated orange zest
75 g (1/3 cup) short-grain rice
125 ml (1/2 cup) cream, whipped
1 teaspoon rose-water
150 g (1 punnet) raspberries
65 g (1/2 cup) raw pistachio kernels, chopped

Bring the milk to the boil in a saucepan with the sugar, orange zest and a pinch of salt. Add the rice, reduce the heat and simmer gently for 30 minutes, stirring occasionally. When the rice has cooked, allow it to cool before folding in the whipped cream and rose-water.

Spoon the rice pudding into serving bowls and top with the raspberries and pistachios. For a wonderful winter dessert, serve the rice pudding with toffee apples (basics) and a little grated lemon zest. Serves 6

vanilla poached white peaches with mint

440 g (2 cups) sugar
2 vanilla beans, spilt lengthways
6 ripe white peaches, cut in half
1 tablespoon lemon juice
20 mint leaves
vanilla ice cream (basics)

Put the sugar and vanilla beans into a large saucepan with 1 litre (4 cups) of water. Bring to the boil and simmer for a few minutes. Put the peaches into the syrup, skin side up, and cook for 2 minutes. With a large spoon, carefully turn the peaches over and cook for a further few minutes. Depending on the size of the peaches, you may have to do this in batches. With the point of a sharp knife, test to see if the peaches are cooked. They should still be firm, but give little resistance to the knife. Remove with a slotted spoon and put into a large bowl. Leave the syrup to reduce for a few minutes. Carefully peel the peaches then pour over the syrup and leave to cool. When the syrup has cooled, add the lemon juice and mint leaves. Serve with vanilla ice cream. Serves 6

fresh and fast

- Bake lengths of rhubarb in the oven with orange juice, brown sugar and a sprinkle of ground ginger. Pile onto a plate and top with chocolate ice cream (basics).
- For a taste of summer in winter, simmer frozen raspberries with some sugar and a small cinnamon quill. When the raspberries have reduced by half, strain them over a bowl. Mould rice pudding in small bowls and upturn onto serving plates. Spoon over the thick and spicy raspberry sauce.
- Place raw pistachio kernels on a baking tray and sprinkle with a little brown sugar. Roast in a 210°C (415°F/Gas 6–7) oven for a few minutes. Remove and roughly chop the nuts when they have cooled. Sprinkle with grated dark chocolate over pancakes (basics) or sliced nectarines and serve with double cream.
- Put halved and stoned peaches on a baking tray. Mix a little softened unsalted butter with finely chopped glacé ginger and brown sugar. Place a little in the centre of each peach and grill (broil) for a few minutes until the butter is bubbling and golden. Serve with vanilla ice cream (basics).

vanilla poached white peaches with mint

apple and blackberry cobbler

250 g (9 oz) plain (all-purpose) flour
8 tablespoons caster (superfine) sugar
1 tablespoon baking powder
60 g (2 1/4 oz) vegetable shortening (copha)
50 g (1 3/4 oz) unsalted butter
1 egg
80 ml (1/3 cup) milk
6 green apples, peeled, cored and cut into eighths
300 g (10 1/2 oz) frozen blackberries
2 tablespoons lemon juice
1 teaspoon cinnamon
whipped cream

Preheat the oven to 210°C (415°F/Gas 6–7). Combine the flour, 1 tablespoon of sugar, baking powder and a pinch of salt in a large bowl. Cut the shortening and butter into small cubes and rub into the flour with your fingertips until the mixture resembles breadcrumbs. Whisk together the egg and milk then stir into the flour mixture until just combined. Turn out the dough onto a floured surface and lightly knead.

Combine the apples, blackberries, 4 tablespoons of sugar, lemon juice and cinnamon and put into a deep baking dish. Break off pieces of the dough and scatter them over the top of the fruit until roughly covered. Sprinkle with the remaining sugar and bake for 40 minutes. Serve with whipped cream. Serves 6

almond and pine nut cake

2 tablespoons unsalted butter
2 mandarins
250 g (9 oz) raw almonds
300 g (10 1/2 oz) caster (superfine) sugar
1/2 teaspoon cinnamon
8 egg whites
85 g (3 oz) plain (all-purpose) flour, sifted
4 tablespoons pine nuts
3 tablespoons dessert wine or Grand Marnier
icing (confectioners') sugar
mandarin salad (basics)
whipped cream

Preheat the oven to 180°C (350°F/Gas 4). Grease a 20 cm (8 in) springform tin with the butter. Peel a mandarin and, with a sharp knife, finely chop the zest. Put 3 tablespoons of zest into a food processor. Add the almonds, sugar and cinnamon and process to a fine consistency. Beat the egg whites with a pinch of salt until stiff peaks form. Lightly fold the almond mixture into the egg whites then add the flour. Spoon the batter into the prepared tin and sprinkle with the pine nuts. Bake for 1 hour, or until a skewer inserted into the centre of the cake comes out clean. Allow to cool before serving.

Pour the dessert wine or Grand Marnier over the cake then dust with icing sugar. Serve with the mandarin salad and cream.

citrus syrup cake

250 g (9 oz) unsalted butter
250 g (9 oz) caster (superfine) sugar
4 eggs
100 g (3 1/2 oz) natural yoghurt
2 lemons, zested and juiced
2 oranges, zested and juiced
2 limes, zested and juiced
250 g (2 cups) self-raising flour
220 g (1 cup) granulated sugar
whipped cream

Preheat the oven to 180°C (350°F/Gas 4). Line a 24 cm (9 1/2 in) springform pan with baking paper. Cream the butter and sugar and then fold in the eggs, yoghurt and citrus zest. Sift in the flour and lightly fold it through the batter. Spoon the batter into the prepared tin. Bake for 45 minutes, or until the cake is golden brown and a skewer inserted into the centre comes out clean. Meanwhile, put the citrus juice into a small saucepan and add the granulated sugar. Bring to the boil and stir until the sugar has dissolved. Remove from the heat.

When the cake is cooked, remove from the oven and prick the top of the cake all over with a skewer. Pour over half the syrup, reserving the rest for serving later. Leave to cool, then serve with reserved syrup and whipped cream. Serves 10

passionfruit curd with pistachio biscotti

5 passionfruit
40 g (1 1/2 oz) unsalted butter
40 g (1 1/2 oz) caster (superfine) sugar
1 whole egg
1 egg yolk
2 teaspoons lime juice
80 ml (1/3 cup) cream, whipped
pistachio biscotti (basics)

Remove the pulp from 3 of the passionfruit and strain through a fine sieve, stirring to push the passionfruit juice through. Discard the strained pulp. Put the juice in a bowl with the unstrained pulp of the remaining passionfruit. Melt the butter in a small saucepan over a low heat. When the butter has just melted, add the sugar, passionfruit pulp, egg and egg yolk. Whisk over a medium heat until the mixture is thick and just boiling. Remove from the heat, stir through the lime juice and refrigerate when cool. Fold through the whipped cream just before serving with pistachio biscotti. Serves 4 to 6

chilli and vanilla syrup with fresh mang

tamarind ginger ice cream with red papaya

chilli and vanilla syrup with fresh mango

220 g (1 cup) sugar
1 vanilla bean, split lengthways
1 large red chilli, seeded and finely chopped
1 lime, juiced
3 mangos, peeled and flesh cut into thick strips
lime sorbet (basics)

Put the sugar, vanilla bean and chilli into a small saucepan with 500 ml (2 cups) of water. Bring to the boil then reduce the heat and allow to simmer for 15 minutes. Allow to cool then stir in the lime juice.

Divide the mango between four chilled bowls and top with scoops of the lime sorbet. Drizzle over the chilli syrup and serve immediately. Serves 4

tamarind ginger ice cream with red papaya

4 egg yolks
145 g (2/3 cup) caster (superfine) sugar
250 ml (1 cup) milk
100 g (1/3 cup) tamarind purée
300 ml (10 1/2 fl oz) cream
110 g (1/2 cup) finely sliced ginger in syrup
2 small ripe red papayas, halved, seeded and peeled

Whisk the yolks and the sugar together in a bowl until they double in volume. Bring the milk to the boil in a saucepan and, when it begins to froth on the surface, pour it into the yolk mixture. Whisk together before returning to the saucepan and placing over a low heat. Stir until the mixture has thickened and coats the back of a wooden spoon. Remove from the heat and strain into a chilled bowl. Stir in the tamarind purée, cream and ginger.

Allow to cool before pouring the mixture into an ice cream machine. Churn according to the manufacturer's instructions. If you don't have an ice cream machine, pour the mixture into a small metal bowl and place in the freezer. Take the ice cream mixture out of the freezer every couple of hours and beat it. This will break up any ice crystals as they form. Serve the ice cream scooped into a red papaya half. Serves 4

nectarine and hazelnut torte

115 g (1/2 cup) caster (superfine) sugar
1 cinnamon quill
1 vanilla bean, split in half lengthways
9 nectarines, quartered
4 eggs
80 g (2 2/3 oz) icing (confectioners') sugar
50 g (1 3/4 oz) plain (all-purpose) flour
3 tablespoons hazelnut meal
30 g (1 oz) butter, melted
whipped cream

Preheat the oven to 180°C (350°F/Gas 4). Put the sugar, cinnamon and vanilla bean into a small saucepan and add 250 ml (1 cup) of water. Bring to the boil then reduce the heat and simmer for 5 minutes. Add the nectarines and cook for 3 minutes. Remove with a slotted spoon and set aside in a bowl. Reduce the syrup by half then pour it over the nectarines. Allow to cool. Put the eggs and icing sugar in a heatproof bowl set over a saucepan of boiling water, making sure the base does not touch the water. Beat until the mixture is just warm then remove from the heat. Continue to beat until it triples in volume. Fold in the flour, hazelnut meal and butter. Spoon into a lined 24 x 34 cm (9 1/2 x 13 1/2 in) sandwich tin. Bake for 20 minutes. Turn out onto a flat surface, cut into large squares and put on dessert plates. Spoon the nectarines over the cake. Top with whipped cream and drizzle with the syrup. Serves 6

fresh and fast

- For a great summertime fruit salad, combine diced red papaya and yellow peaches with passionfruit and lime juice. Sweeten with palm sugar if desired. Serve with lime sorbet (basics).
- Poach nectarines in a light syrup spiced with cinnamon, cardamom and star anise. Serve with caramel ice cream.
- Finely dice mango cheeks and put into a bowl with finely sliced strawberries and halved blueberries. Finely slice some mint leaves and add to the fruit salsa. Spoon over lime sorbet (basics).
- Lightly roast hazelnuts, rub away any of the bitter dark skin and roughly chop. Finely dice several pieces of Turkish delight and put into a bowl with the hazelnuts. Stir in softened chocolate ice cream (basics). Refreeze the ice cream and then serve with fresh strawberries.

nectarine and hazelnut torte

chocolate nut meringues with cream and berries

From shiny purple blueberries to lush ripe raspberries — all they need is a sprinkle of sugar.

frozen raspberry whip with strawberries

chocolate nut meringues with cream and berries

3 egg whites
200 g (7 oz) caster (superfine) sugar
2 tablespoons dark cocoa
2 tablespoons ground hazelnuts
50 g (1 3/4 oz) flaked almonds
150 ml (5 fl oz) cream, whipped
500 g (1 lb 2 oz) mixed berries

Preheat the oven to 150°C (300°F/Gas 2). Line a large baking tray with baking paper. Whisk the egg whites until they form soft peaks and then slowly add the sugar, continuing to beat until the mixture is white and glossy. Fold in the cocoa and ground hazelnuts, then spoon the meringue into 6 large dollops on the tray. Using the back of the spoon, create a dip in the top of each meringue. Sprinkle with the almonds and bake for 45 minutes. Turn off the heat, but leave the meringues to cool in the oven with the door ajar. Store in an airtight container until ready to use. Serve topped with whipped cream and berries. Serves 6

frozen raspberry whip with strawberries

150 g (1 punnet) raspberries
1 teaspoon lemon juice
115 g (1/2 cup) caster (superfine) sugar
1 egg white
500 g (2 punnets) strawberries
1 tablespoon icing (confectioners') sugar

Whip the raspberries, lemon juice, sugar and egg white with electric beaters for 10 minutes, or until the mixture is light and fluffy and has tripled in size. Spoon into a container and put into the freezer for several hours or overnight until it is frozen. Just prior to serving, hull and halve the strawberries, reserving some whole ones for serving. Sprinkle the strawberry halves with the icing sugar and lightly toss until they are well coated. Set aside for 5 minutes before serving with a scoop of the frozen raspberry whip. Serves 4 to 6

figs in sauterne with crème fraîche parfait

spiced yoghurt with fresh fruit

figs in sauterne with crème fraîche parfait

12 fresh figs, halved
400 ml (14 fl oz) sauterne
1 teaspoon honey
5 egg yolks
125 g (4 1/2 oz) caster (superfine) sugar
1 teaspoon natural vanilla extract
500 ml (2 cups) crème fraîche

Put the figs in a bowl and cover with the sauterne. Drizzle with honey then cover and refrigerate for 12 hours or overnight.

Whisk the egg yolks, sugar and vanilla extract until the mixture is thick and very pale. Fold through the crème fraîche then spoon into a 8 x 22 cm (3 x 9 in) tin lined with baking paper. Freeze until firm. Slice the parfait into 6 thick slices and serve on chilled plates with the halved figs and a spoonful of the sauterne. Serves 6

spiced yoghurt with fresh fruit

2 cinnamon sticks
2 star anise
2 cloves
2 vanilla beans, split lengthways
2 cardamom pods, split lengthways
250 ml (1 cup) cream
1 tablespoon sugar
300 g (10 1/2 oz) Greek-style yoghurt
fresh fruit

Put the cinnamon, star anise, cloves, vanilla beans, cardamom pods and cream into a small saucepan over a low heat. Allow to simmer for 30 minutes. Remove from the heat, strain, then stir in the sugar before allowing to cool. Fold the spiced cream through the yoghurt and serve drizzled over fresh fruit or salads such as the pomegranate and fig salad or a Middle Eastern fruit salad (basics). Serves 6

cinnamon quince with orange mascarpone

3 quinces
185 ml (3/4 cup) red wine
125 ml (1/2 cup) fresh orange juice
4 tablespoons brown sugar
1 cinnamon quill
orange mascarpone (basics)

Preheat the oven to 180°C (350°F/Gas 4). Peel and core the quinces and slice into eighths. Put into a baking dish and cover with the red wine, orange juice, brown sugar and cinnamon. Add 250 ml (1 cup) of water and cover with foil. Bake for 2 hours. Remove the foil and turn the quince pieces over so that they are well coated in the liquid. Return to the oven and bake for another hour, or until the liquid has reduced to a syrup.

Divide between four plates and serve with a dollop of orange mascarpone and a drizzle of the quince syrup. For a richer wintertime dessert, serve the quince with thick slices of gingerbread (basics). Serves 4

fresh and fast

- Marinate thickly sliced white peaches in sauterne with a pinch of ground cloves. Serve with thick creamy custard (basics) or sweet mascarpone.
- Slice figs in half and sprinkle with some finely grated ginger and a little ground cinnamon. Drizzle with maple syrup and bake in a 210°C (415°F/Gas 6–7) oven for 10 minutes. Serve with vanilla ice cream and almond bread.
- Stir quince paste through soft goat's curd with a splash of Grand Marnier. Spoon onto a serving plate and cover with toasted flaked almonds. Serve with fresh berries or sliced nectarines.
- Toss thickly sliced bananas in a little lime juice and cinnamon or lemon and cointreau syrup then serve with the spiced yoghurt.

It's impossible not to be tempted by the sultry flavours of dark chocolate, vanilla and cardamom

chocolate pots

300 ml (10 1/2 fl oz) single cream
200 g (7 oz) dark chocolate, roughly chopped
1/2 teaspoon natural vanilla extract
1/2 teaspoon ground cardamom
1 egg

Melt the cream and chocolate in a double boiler or over a low heat. Allow the chocolate to melt, stirring occasionally. Add a pinch of salt with the vanilla and cardamom and finally whisk in the egg. Continue to whisk over a gentle heat until smooth. Pour the mixture into six 125 ml (1/2 cup) pots and chill for 3 hours. Serve with fresh berries and the chocolate wafers. Serves 6

chocolate wafers

50 g (1 3/4 oz) caster (superfine) sugar
50 g (1 3/4 oz) unsalted butter, softened
2 egg whites
40 g (1 1/2 oz) plain (all-purpose) flour
10 g (1/4 oz) dark cocoa

Preheat the oven to 180°C (350°F/Gas 4). Whisk the sugar and butter until it is light and creamy. Slowly add the egg whites and then the flour and cocoa. Chill for 1 hour.

Line a baking sheet with baking paper and, using the back of a spoon, spread 1 tablespoon of the mixture into a thin 10 cm (4 in) circle. Repeat, leaving a little space between wafers. Bake for 15 minutes. Remove from the oven and carefully lift the wafers from the tray with a spatula. Allow to cool on a wire rack. Makes 12

cumin and lime cookies

6 tablespoons unsalted butter
150 g (5 1/2 oz) caster (superfine) sugar
1 teaspoon ground cumin
1 teaspoon natural vanilla extract
2 tablespoons of lime juice plus the grated zest of 1 lime
1 egg
150 g (5 1/2 oz) plain (all-purpose) flour
1 teaspoon baking powder
whipped cream
fresh fruit

Preheat the oven to 180°C (350°F/Gas 4). Cream the butter and sugar then fold in the cumin, vanilla, lime juice, lime zest and egg. Sift in the flour and baking powder and stir together. Spoon the batter onto a baking sheet lined with baking paper — use 1 heaped tablespoon of mixture per biscuit. Bake for 12 minutes, or until golden brown and allow to cool on a wire rack.

Serve with whipped cream and slices of ripe fruit such as figs, nectarines and peaches. Makes 20 large biscuits

chocolate marquise

lime syrup puddings

4 tablespoons golden syrup
3 tablespoons lime juice
1 lime, zested
2 eggs, separated
125 g (4 1/2 oz) unsalted butter
115 g (1/2 cup) dark brown sugar
1 teaspoon natural vanilla extract
155 g (1 1/4 cups) plain (all-purpose) flour
1 1/2 teaspoons ground ginger
1 teaspoon cream of tartar
1/2 teaspoon bicarbonate of soda
125 ml (1/2 cup) milk
pouring cream

Preheat the oven to 180°C (350°F/Gas 4). Grease six 150 ml (5 fl oz) ramekins. Mix the golden syrup, lime juice and zest together in a small bowl. Divide the mixture between the moulds. Beat the egg whites until stiff and then set to one side. Cream the butter and sugar together then add the egg yolks and vanilla. Fold in the flour, ginger, cream of tartar and bicarbonate of soda alternately with the milk. Lightly fold through the beaten egg whites. Spoon the batter into the ramekins and cover with circles of baking paper. Put the ramekins into a baking tray and fill with water until it reaches halfway up the sides of the ramekins. Bake for 40 minutes, or until the puddings are cooked through. Upturn the puddings onto six plates and drizzle with cream. Serves 6

blood plum and cinnamon jellies

6 blood plums, quartered and stoned
230 g (1 cup) caster (superfine) sugar
1 cinnamon quill
1 vanilla bean, split in half lengthways
1–2 oranges, juiced
6 gelatine leaves
pouring cream

Put the plums, sugar, cinnamon quill, vanilla bean and 750 ml (3 cups) of water into a saucepan. Bring to the boil and then reduce the heat. Continue to simmer for 30 minutes. Remove from the heat and strain the plum syrup through a very fine sieve or muslin. Pour the syrup into a measuring jug and add enough orange juice to make 600 ml (21 fl oz) of plum syrup. Soak the gelatine leaves in a large bowl of cold water for 10 to 15 minutes, or until very soft. Return the syrup to the saucepan and put over a low heat until the syrup is warm. Squeeze any excess liquid from the gelatine and add it to the warm syrup. Pour the jelly into six 100 ml (3 1/2 fl oz) moulds and put in the refrigerator for 3 hours or overnight, until set. Serve with a drizzle of cream. Serves 6

chocolate marquise

100 g (3 1/2 oz) dark chocolate
50 g (1 3/4 oz) unsalted butter, softened
50 g (1 3/4 oz) caster (superfine) sugar
2 tablespoons unsweetened cocoa powder
2 egg yolks
1 teaspoon rose-water
150 ml (5 fl oz) cream
150 g (1 punnet) raspberries
6 white nectarines, sliced
45 g (1/2 cup) flaked almonds, toasted
icing (confectioners') sugar

Melt the chocolate in a heat-proof bowl set over a saucepan of boiling water, making sure the base does not touch the water. Beat the butter with half the sugar until pale and fluffy. Mix in the cocoa. Beat the yolks with the remaining sugar until pale and smooth, then add the rose-water. Whip the cream until thick. Mix the melted chocolate into the butter mixture, fold in the egg mixture, then fold in the cream. Spoon into a lined 8 x 22 cm (3 x 9 in) tin and chill for 3 hours, or until set.

Turn out the marquise and cut into thick slices. Serve with raspberries, white nectarines, toasted flaked almonds and a dusting of icing sugar. Serves 4 to 6

fresh and fast

- Fill sweet pastry cases with a little mascarpone and top with sugary berries. Drizzle with sweet liqueur or cardamom and rose-water syrup and serve immediately.
- Stew plums in red wine until they are just soft. Remove with a slotted spoon and serve with Greek-style yoghurt, a drizzle of honey and cardamom rose-water syrup.
- Quarter and stone plums and put them in the base of a baking dish. Sprinkle with sugar, ground ginger and cinnamon. Put 125 g (1 cup) plain (all-purpose) flour and 90 g (1 cup) desiccated coconut in a bowl and rub in a little unsalted butter until it forms crumbs. Sprinkle over the plums and bake at 180°C (350°F/Gas 4) until the crumble is golden brown. Serve with thick (double/heavy) cream.
- The easiest dessert in the world? A large platter piled with whole strawberries and a large block of milk chocolate.

blood plum and cinnamon jellies

basics

lemon mayonnaise

2 egg yolks
1 lemon, zested and juiced
250 ml (1 cup) oil
sea salt

Whisk the egg yolks, lemon zest and juice together in a large bowl. Slowly drizzle in the oil while whisking until the mixture thickens, and keep whisking the mixture until it becomes thick and creamy. Season to taste with the salt. If the mixture is very thick, add a little cold water until you achieve the right consistency.

roast sweet potato

2 large orange sweet potatoes (kumara)
3 tablespoons olive oil
sea salt

Preheat the oven to 180°C (350°F/Gas 4). Peel the sweet potatoes and cut them into chunks. Toss the potatoes in the oil and season with a good sprinkling of sea salt and some freshly ground black pepper.

Spread the potatoes out on a baking tray in a single layer and roast them for 30 minutes or until they are browned and cooked through. Serves 4

basic vinaigrette

2 tablespoons vinegar
125 ml (1/2 cup) olive oil
1 teaspoon Dijon mustard

Whisk all the ingredients together and season to taste. You may like to add other flavours, such as fresh thyme, basil or rosemary. The vinegar can be replaced with lemon juice.

tapenade

75 g (1/2 cup) pitted black olives
1 garlic clove
15 g (1/2 cup) roughly chopped flat-leaf (Italian) parsley leaves
10 basil leaves
2 anchovy fillets
1 teaspoon capers
125 ml (1/2 cup) olive oil

Put all the ingredients except the oil in a blender or food processor and blend to a rough paste. Add the oil in a stream until you reach the desired consistency. Season with freshly ground black pepper to taste.

pesto

150 g (1 bunch) basil, leaves removed
140 g (1 bunch) flat-leaf (Italian) parsley, roughly chopped
100 g (1 cup) grated Parmesan cheese
1 garlic clove
80 g (1/2 cup) pine nuts, toasted
170 ml (2/3 cup) olive oil

Put the basil, parsley, Parmesan, garlic and pine nuts into a food processor, or use a pestle and mortar, and blend or pound the mixture to make a thick paste.

Add the oil in a steady stream until the paste has a spoonable consistency.

To keep the pesto, put it in a sterilized jar and add a layer of olive oil on top. This will prevent the surface of the pesto oxidizing and turning brown. Keep the pesto in the fridge for up to 2 weeks.

croutons

6 pieces thick-sliced white bread
125 ml (1/2 cup) oil

Remove the crusts from the bread and cut it into small cubes. Heat the oil in a frying pan and, when the surface of the oil starts to shimmer, add the cubes of bread and reduce the heat. Toss the bread in the oil until the croutons are golden brown.

Remove the croutons with a slotted spoon and drain them on paper towels. Season with sea salt and freshly ground black pepper.

tomato sauce

6 Roma (plum) tomatoes
10 basil leaves
1 teaspoon sugar
1 garlic clove
2 tablespoons extra virgin olive oil
1 teaspoon balsamic vinegar

Preheat the oven to 200°C (400°F/Gas 6). Put the tomatoes on a baking tray and roast them in the oven until their skins are beginning to blacken all over.

Put the tomatoes into a food processor or blender with the basil leaves, sugar, garlic, olive oil and vinegar. Blend to form a thick sauce, thinning the mixture with a little warm water if necessary. This will keep for 2 to 3 days in the fridge.

shortcrust pastry

200 g (1 2/3 cups) plain (all-purpose flour)
100 g (3 1/2 oz) chilled unsalted butter

Put the flour, butter and a pinch of salt into a food processor and process for 1 minute. Add 2 tablespoons of chilled water and process until the mixture comes together. Wrap the dough in plastic wrap and chill for 30 minutes.

Roll the pastry out as thinly as possible* and line a greased 25 cm (10 in) tart tin or six 8 cm (3 in) tartlet tins. Chill for a further 30 minutes. Prick the base, line it with crumpled baking paper and fill with rice or baking weights. Place the tin in a preheated 180°C (350°F/Gas 4) oven for 10 to 15 minutes or until the pastry looks cooked and dry. Remove and allow to cool. Makes 1 tart case**

* The easiest way to do this is to roll it out between two layers of plastic wrap.

** Tart cases that are not used immediately can be stored in the freezer for several weeks. Put the tart case in a preheated oven direct from the freezer (there's no need to thaw the case first).

tamarind water

100 g (3 1/2 oz) tamarind pulp

To make tamarind water, put the tamarind pulp in a bowl and cover it with 500 ml (2 cups) of boiling water. Allow it to steep for 1 hour, stirring occasionally to break up the fibres, then strain.

buttered couscous

200 g (1 cup) instant couscous
2 tablespoons butter

Bring 250 ml (1 cup) water to the boil in a saucepan and throw in the couscous. Take the pan off the heat, add the butter in small pieces and leave it to stand for 10 minutes.

Fluff up the couscous with a fork and season well with salt and black pepper. Serves 4

basic polenta

350 g (2 1/3 cups) polenta
100 g (3 1/2 oz) butter, cut into cubes
100 g (3 1/2 oz) grated Parmesan cheese

Bring 2 litres (8 cups) of water and a teaspoon of sea salt to the boil in a large saucepan. Lower the heat to a simmer and slowly add the polenta in a steady stream, stirring with a whisk to blend it smoothly. Reduce the heat to low and, stirring occasionally, allow the polenta to cook for half an hour. The polenta is cooked when it begins to pull away from the sides of the saucepan. Stir in the butter and Parmesan and serve immediately. Season with sea salt and freshly ground black pepper.

rouille

1 thick slice sourdough bread
1 pinch saffron threads
1 red capsicum (pepper), roasted and skinned
1/4 teaspoon paprika
2 garlic cloves
125 ml (1/2 cup) light olive oil

Tear the bread into pieces and put it in a bowl. Bring the saffron threads and 60 ml (1/4 cup) of water to the boil in a small saucepan and simmer for a minute. Pour the hot saffron water over the bread.

Allow the bread to soak in the water and then add it to a food processor or blender with the capsicum, paprika and garlic. Blend to form a smooth paste, then add the olive oil in a stream to give a thick consistency. Season with salt to taste.

mashed potato

4 large floury potatoes, peeled
2 tablespoons milk
2 tablespoons butter

Cut the potatoes into pieces and cook them in simmering water for 15 minutes, or until they are soft. Drain them well, put them back in the pan with the milk and butter and mash them until they are smooth. Season with salt and pepper. Serves 4

pizza dough

1 sachet (7 g) dried yeast
1 teaspoon caster (superfine) sugar
250 g (2 cups) plain (all-purpose) flour
1 egg, beaten
50 ml (1 3/4 fl oz) milk
1 tablespoon olive oil

Place the yeast, sugar and 75 ml (1/3 cup) of warm water into a small bowl and stir lightly to combine. Set aside for 10 to 15 minutes or until it begins to froth up. Sift the flour into a bowl and make a well in the centre. Add the egg, milk and 1 teaspoon of sea salt. Add the frothy yeast mixture and gradually work the ingredients together to form a stiff dough. Turn out onto a floured surface and knead until smooth and elastic. Oil a bowl with a little olive oil and place the dough in it. Rub any remaining oil over the dough before covering it with a damp cloth and placing it somewhere warm to rise. The dough should double in size in about 2 to 3 hours.

curry spice blend

1 teaspoon cumin seeds
1 teaspoon coriander seeds
1 teaspoon mustard seeds
1/4 teaspoon fennel seeds
1/2 cinnamon stick
1/2 teaspoon black peppercorns
1 teaspoon ground turmeric

Toast the cumin and coriander seeds until aromatic then place all the spices in a spice grinder and grind to a fine powder.

tomato rice

1 tablespoon sesame oil
1 onion, finely diced
1 garlic clove, crushed
3 ripe tomatoes, diced
200 g (1 cup) basmati rice

Put the sesame oil into a large saucepan over a medium heat. Add the onion and garlic and cook until the onion is soft and transparent. Add the tomatoes, rice and 1/2 teaspoon of sea salt and stir for a minute before adding 375 ml (1 1/2 cups) of water. Raise the heat and bring the rice to the boil. Cover the saucepan with a lid and reduce the heat to low. Leave covered for 20 minutes and then remove from the heat.

curry sauce

60 g (2 1/4 oz) butter
1 red onion, finely diced
1 garlic clove, crushed
2 teaspoons grated fresh ginger
1 teaspoon ground turmeric
1 teaspoon ground cumin
10 saffron threads
1 tablespoon tomato paste (purée)
250 ml (1 cup) white wine

Melt the butter in a heavy-based frying pan and fry the onion, garlic and ginger until the onion is soft and transparent. Add all the spices and fry for a further minute. Add the tomato paste and white wine and allow to simmer until it has reduced by half. Delicious served with grilled meat.

aioli

2 egg yolks
2 large garlic cloves, crushed
300 ml (10 1/2 fl oz) olive oil
1 lemon, juiced
1/4 teaspoon ground white pepper

Whisk together the egg yolks and garlic with a little sea salt. Begin to add the olive oil in a thin stream, whisking continuously. Add a little of the lemon juice and then continue with the remaining oil. Fold in the remaining lemon juice and season to taste with the white pepper and a little sea salt.

tahini sauce

135 g (1/2 cup) tahini
1 lemon, juiced
2 tablespoons natural yoghurt
1 teaspoon ground cumin

Combine the tahini into a bowl and add the lemon juice, yoghurt, cumin and 3 tablespoons of water. Stir to combine. Serve as a dressing for fish, chicken or with spiced salads.

horseradish gremolata

3 tablespoons finely chopped flat-leaf (Italian) parsley
1 tablespoon finely grated lemon rind
1 tablespoon finely grated fresh horseradish root

Mix all the ingredients together in a bowl and serve scattered over osso bucco or seared lamb backstrap just before serving.

Vietnamese dipping sauce (nuoc cham)

1 tablespoon sugar
1 1/2 tablespoons fish sauce
2 tablespoons lime juice
1/2 garlic clove, finely minced
1 small red chilli, seeded and finely chopped

Put the sugar in a small bowl and add 2 tablespoons of hot water. Stir until the sugar is well dissolved. Add the remaining ingredients and stir well. Allow to cool then serve with fish cakes, fresh spring rolls or drizzle over grilled fish.

harissa

2 red capsicums (peppers)
3 red chillies
2 garlic cloves
1 tablespoon cumin seeds, roasted and ground
1 tablespoon coriander (cilantro) seeds, roasted and ground
30 g (1 cup) coriander (cilantro) leaves
1 tablespoon pomegranate molasses
2 1/2 tablespoons olive oil

Preheat the oven to 210°C (415°F/Gas 6–7). Put the capsicums in a baking tray and bake until the skin is blistered and blackened. Remove and set aside to cool. When cool, remove the skin and seeds from the capsicums and put the flesh in a food processor with the chillies, garlic, ground cumin and coriander, pomegranate molasses and 1 teaspoon of sea salt. Blend to a purée then add the olive oil and process again.

sesame crisps

1 egg
80 g (1/2 cup) sesame seeds
250 ml (1 cup) peanut oil
8 won ton wrappers

Whisk the egg and 1 tablespoon of water in a small bowl. Put the sesame seeds in another small bowl.

Heat the oil in a deep frying pan or wok over a high heat. Brush the egg wash onto one of the wrappers then sprinkle with the sesame seeds. When the oil is hot, add the won ton and fry for 30 seconds, or until it is puffed and golden brown. Remove the wrapper from the pan and drain on paper towels. Repeat with the remaining wrappers.

vegetable stock

2 onions, roughly chopped
2 leeks, sliced
2 tablespoons olive oil
3 carrots, sliced
3 celery stalks, sliced
2 parsnips, sliced
150 g (1 bunch) flat-leaf (Italian) parsley
2 garlic cloves
6 peppercorns
4 sprigs thyme

Heat a large saucepan over a high heat and add the onions, leeks and olive oil.

Stir until the onions begin to soften, then add the carrots, celery, parsnips and 3 litres (12 cups) of cold water. Add the remaining ingredients and bring to a simmering heat. Continue to simmer for 3 hours. Remove from the heat and strain into a large bowl. Using the back of a large spoon, press the vegetables into the strainer to draw out most of the flavour.

dashi stock

30 g (1 oz) dried kombu
20 g (3/4 oz) bonito flakes

Put 2 litres (8 cups) of cold water and the kombu in a saucepan and slowly bring it to the boil over a medium heat. Regulate the heat so that the water takes around 10 minutes to come to the boil. As it nears boiling point, test the thickest part of the seaweed: if it is soft to the touch and your thumbnail easily cuts into the surface, remove the kombu.

Let the water come back to the boil, then add half a glass of cold water and pour in the bonito flakes. As soon as the stock returns to the boil, remove it from the heat and skim the surface. When the bonito flakes have sunk to the bottom of the pan, strain the stock through a square of muslin or a very fine sieve. The finished stock should be clear and free of bonito flakes.

* Instant dashi is available in most large supermarkets, health food stores or specialty Asian shops.

veal stock

1 kg (2 lb) veal bones (ask the butcher to cut into small pieces)
2 tablespoons olive oil
2 onions, sliced
3 garlic cloves, minced
2 leeks, roughly chopped
2 celery sticks, sliced
2 large tomatoes, roughly chopped
1 bay leaf
6 peppercorns

Preheat the oven to 200°C (400°F/Gas 6). Put the veal bones and olive oil into a large baking dish and bake for 30 minutes. Add the vegetables and continue to bake until the bones are well browned. Put the roasted bones and vegetables in a large saucepan and cover generously with cold water. Bring to the boil, then reduce the heat to a simmer. Skim any fat from the surface then add the bay leaf and peppercorns. Maintain the heat at a low simmer for 4 hours. Strain the stock into a bowl and allow to cool. Using a large spoon, remove any fat that has risen to the surface. Return the stock to a saucepan and simmer over a low heat to reduce and concentrate the flavour.

chicken stock

1 chicken carcass, chopped
1 onion, sliced
1 carrot, sliced
2 sticks celery, sliced
1 leek, roughly chopped
1 bay leaf
a few parsley stalks
6 peppercorns

Put the chicken bones into a large saucepan and cover with 2 litres (8 cups) of cold water. Bring to the boil, then reduce the heat to a simmer. Skim any fat from the surface then add remaining ingredients. Maintain the heat at a low simmer for 3 hours. Strain the stock into a bowl and allow to cool. Using a large spoon, remove any fat that has risen to the surface. Return the stock to a saucepan and simmer over a low heat to reduce and concentrate the flavour.

quince paste

6 quinces, quartered
1 lemon, juiced
sugar

Put the quinces into a saucepan with the lemon juice and 250 ml (1 cup) of water.

Bring to the boil and then simmer for 30 minutes. Remove from the heat when the quinces are soft and then strain the fruit through a food mill. Weigh the fruit purée and return it to a saucepan with three-quarters of its weight in sugar. Simmer over a very low heat, stirring occasionally, until the mixture thickens. This may take 2 to 3 hours. When the mixture is quite thick pour into a container and allow to cool.

lime sorbet

250 g (1 cup) sugar
4–5 limes

Dissolve 1 litre (4 cups) of water and sugar together in a saucepan over a low heat. Once dissolved, boil for 2 to 3 minutes before removing from the heat and allowing to cool.

Finely grate the rind of 1 lime and add it to the sugar syrup with the juice of 4 limes. Taste and then add a little more lime juice if you think it is necessary. When the syrup has cooled, put in an ice cream machine and churn following the manufacturer's instructions.

orange mascarpone

2 eggs, separated
2 tablespoons sugar
1 tablespoon grated orange rind
250 g (9 oz) mascarpone
1 tablespoon Grand Marnier

Beat the egg whites until they are stiff. Set aside. Beat the egg yolks with the sugar and grated orange rind and, when light and creamy, gently whisk in the mascarpone and Grand Marnier. Fold the egg whites through the mascarpone and chill for 1 hour.

vanilla ice cream

8 egg yolks
200 g (7 oz) caster (superfine) sugar
375 ml ($1\frac{1}{2}$ cups) milk
375 ml ($1\frac{1}{2}$ cups) cream
1 vanilla bean, split

Whisk together the egg yolks and sugar until thick and creamy. Put the milk and cream in a saucepan with the split vanilla bean. Bring the milk just to the boil, then pour the hot milk into the sugar and egg mixture while still whisking.

Pour the custard back into the saucepan and continue to stir over a low heat until the custard is thick enough to coat the back of a wooden spoon. Take out the vanilla bean and scrape the seeds into the mixture.

Put the cooled mixture into an ice cream maker and churn following the manufacturer's instructions. Alternatively, put it in a freezer-proof box and freeze. Take the ice cream mixture out of the freezer every couple of hours and beat it. This will break up any ice crystals as they form and make the ice cream creamier.

chocolate ice cream

6 egg yolks
100 g ($3\frac{1}{2}$ oz) caster sugar
300 ml ($10\frac{1}{2}$ fl oz) milk
300 ml ($10\frac{1}{2}$ fl oz) cream
300 g ($10\frac{1}{2}$ oz) dark chocolate, broken into pieces

Whisk together the egg yolks and sugar until thick and creamy. Put the milk and cream in a saucepan with the split vanilla bean. Bring the milk just to the boil, then pour the hot milk into the sugar and egg mixture while still whisking.

Pour the custard back into the saucepan and continue to stir over a low heat until the custard is thick enough to coat the back of a wooden spoon. Remove from the heat and add the chocolate, stirring until melted.

Put the cooled mixture into an ice cream maker and churn following the manufacturer's instructions.

toffee apples

4 green apples, peeled, cored and cut into eighths
3 tablespoons caster (superfine) sugar
1 teaspoon ground cinnamon

Toss the apple pieces with the sugar, cinnamon and 2 tablespoons of water.

Tip them into a heavy-based frying pan over a medium heat and let them caramelize and brown. Turn each of the apple pieces as they begin to caramelize and take them out when they are cooked on both sides.

cardamom almond bread

3 egg whites
80 g ($\frac{1}{3}$ cup) caster (superfine) sugar
85 g ($\frac{2}{3}$ cup) plain (all-purpose) flour
2 oranges, zested
90 g ($\frac{1}{2}$ cup) blanched almonds
$\frac{1}{4}$ teaspoon ground cardamom

Preheat the oven to 180°C (350°F/Gas 4). To make the almond bread, oil an 8 x 22 cm (3 x 9 in) loaf tin and line it with baking paper. Whip the egg whites until they are stiff and then slowly whisk in the sugar. When the sugar has been fully incorporated and the whites are glossy, fold in the flour, orange zest, almonds and cardamom. Spoon the mixture into the prepared tin and bake it for 40 minutes.

Cool the almond bread on a wire rack. When it is cold, cut it into thin slices with a serrated knife and spread the slices out on a baking tray. Bake at 140°C (275°F/Gas 1) for 15 minutes or until the slices are crisp. Allow them to cool completely on a wire rack before storing them in an airtight container.

pancake mix

125 g (1 cup) self-raising flour
1 teaspoon caster (superfine) sugar
1 egg
185 ml ($\frac{2}{3}$ cup) milk

Blend the flour, sugar, egg and a pinch of salt together in a large bowl to form a thick batter, then slowly whisk in the milk. Make sure you remove any lumps as you whisk. Cover the mixture and put it in the fridge until you are ready to use it.

pistachio biscotti

125 g (1 cup) plain (all-purpose) flour
115 g (1/2 cup) caster sugar
1 teaspoon baking powder
150 g (1 cup) shelled pistachios
2 teaspoons grated orange rind
2 eggs, beaten

Preheat the oven to 180°C (350°F/Gas 4). Mix the flour, sugar, baking powder, pistachios and orange zest together in a large bowl. Make a well in the centre and fold in the eggs to make a sticky dough Turn out onto a clean floured surface. Divide the dough into 2 sections and roll out each portion to form a log approximately 4 cm (1 1/2 in) in length. Place the logs onto a baking tray lined with baking paper, leaving space between each log to spread a little. Bake for 30 minutes. Remove and allow to cool. Reduce the oven temperature to 140°C (275°F/Gas 1). With a sharp bread knife, cut each of the loaves into thin slices approximately 5 mm (1/4 in) wide. Lay the biscuits on a baking tray and return them to the oven. Bake for 20 minutes turning the biscuits once. Remove from the oven and cool on wire racks. Makes 30 to 40 biscuits.

custard

2 egg yolks
2 tablespoons caster (superfine) sugar
310 ml (1 1/4 cups) milk
1 vanilla bean, split

Whisk together the egg yolks and sugar until thick and creamy. Put the milk in a saucepan with the split vanilla bean. Bring the milk just to the boil, then pour the hot milk into the sugar and egg mixture while still whisking.

Pour the custard back into the saucepan and continue to stir over a low heat until the custard is thick enough to coat the back of a wooden spoon. Take out the vanilla bean and scrape the seeds into the mixture.

cardamom and rose-water syrup

110 g (1/2 cup) sugar
1 teaspoon lemon juice
5 cardamom pods, lightly crushed
1/2 teaspoon rose-water

Put the sugar, lemon juice and cardamom pods in a small saucepan and add 250 ml (1 cup) of water. Bring slowly to the boil, making sure that the sugar dissolves completely, then reduce the heat and simmer the mixture for 5 minutes.

Remove the syrup from the heat and stir in the rose-water. This syrup will keep for a couple of weeks in the fridge.

chocolate tart case

160 g (5 1/2 oz) unsalted butter
185 g (1 1/2 cups) plain (all-purpose) flour
2 tablespoons cocoa powder

Put all the ingredients in a food processor and whiz to form a paste. If the pastry doesn't ball together, add a dash of chilled water. Cover the pastry in plastic wrap and put it in the fridge for half an hour.

Roll the pastry out as thinly as possible* and use it to line a 25 cm (10 in) tart tin. Chill the pastry until it is ready to use.

To bake, preheat the oven to 180°C (350°F/Gas 4). Cover the pastry with a layer of crumpled baking paper weighted down with baking weights, dried beans or raw rice and put it in the oven for 15 minutes.

Remove the paper and weights and bake for a further 5 minutes or until the base of the pastry is cooked through and looks dry. Makes 1 tart case

* The easiest way to do this is to roll it out between two layers of plastic wrap.

lemon and cointreau syrup

3 lemons, juiced
60 g (1/4 cup) sugar
1 star anise
2 tablespoons Cointreau

Put the lemon juice, sugar and star anise in a small saucepan. Bring to the boil, then reduce the heat, allowing the mixture to simmer for a few minutes. Remove from the heat and let it cool before adding the Cointreau. This syrup will keep for a couple of weeks in the fridge.

poaching syrup for fruit

Place 2 parts water to 1 part sugar in a saucepan and heat over a medium heat until the sugar has dissolved. Add flavourings such as cinnamon, lemon peel or wine and poach fruit

pomegranate and fig salad

6 green figs, skin removed
2 guava
3 oranges, segmented
2 pomegranates

Finely slice the figs and guavas and put in a bowl with the orange segments. Slice the pomegranates in half and scoop out the seeds into the bowl. Squeeze any remaining juice from the pomegranates over the salad.

mandarin salad

6 mandarins
1/2 teaspoon orange flower water

Segment 4 of the mandarins and place into a bowl. Squeeze the juice from the remaining two mandarins over the segments and add the orange flower water. Add half a teaspoon of finely chopped mandarin rind and stir together.

middle-eastern fruit salad

70 g (2 1/4 oz) dried figs
70 g (2 1/4 oz) dried apricots
70 g (2 1/4 oz) pitted prunes
55 g (1/4 cup) granulated sugar
55 g (1/4 cup) orange juice
1 teaspoon rose-water

Cut the dried fruit into bite-sized pieces and place in a small bowl. Place the sugar, 250 ml (1 cup) of water and the orange juice in a small saucepan and bring to the boil over a medium heat, stirring to dissolve the sugar.

Remove from the heat and stir in the rose-water. Pour the liquid over the dried fruit and allow to soak for several hours.

gingerbread

125 g (4 oz) butter
115 g (1/2 cup) sugar
90 g (1/4 cup) molasses
1 egg
175 g (6 oz) plain (all-purpose) flour
1 teaspoon baking powder
2 teaspoons ground ginger
1/2 teaspoon ground cinnamon
2 tablespoons preserved ginger in syrup, grated
60 ml (1/4 cup) brandy

Preheat the oven to 170°C (325°F/Gas 3). Line a 23 x 13 x 7 cm (9 x 5 x 3 in) loaf tin. Beat together the sugar and butter until light and fluffy. Beat in the molasses and egg. Work in the dry ingredients and then fold through the ginger and brandy. Pour into the tin and bake for 1 hour 45 minutes or when a skewer inserted into the centre of the cake comes out clean. Serve in thick slices with cream.

sweet shortcrust tart case

200 g (1 2/3 cups) plain (all-purpose) flour
100 g (3 1/2 oz) unsalted butter
1 tablespoon caster (superfine) sugar

Put the flour, butter, sugar and a pinch of salt into a food processor and process for 1 minute. Add 2 tablespoons of chilled water and process until the mixture comes together. Wrap the dough in plastic wrap and chill for 30 minutes.

Roll the pastry out as thinly as possible* and line a greased 25 cm (10 in) tart tin or six 8 cm (3 in) tartlet tins. Chill for a further 30 minutes. Prick the base, line it with crumpled baking paper and fill with rice or baking weights. Place the tin in a preheated 180°C (350°F/Gas 4) oven for 10 to 15 minutes or until the pastry looks cooked and dry. Remove and allow to cool. Makes 1 tart case**

* The easiest way to do this is to roll it out between two layers of plastic wrap.

** Tart cases that are not used immediately can be stored in the freezer for several weeks. Put the tart case in a preheated oven direct from the freezer (there's no need to thaw the case first).

glossary

balsamic vinegar

Balsamic vinegar is a dark, fragrant, sweetish aged vinegar made from grape juice. The production of authentic balsamic vinegar is carefully controlled. Bottles of the real thing have 'Aceto Balsamico Tradizionale de Modena' written on the label, while commercial varieties simply have 'Aceto Balsamico de Modena'.

bamboo steamer

This inexpensive woven bamboo container has a lid and a slatted base. Food is put inside the container and then placed over a saucepan of boiling water to cook. Bamboo steamers are available from Asian grocery stores and most large supermarkets.

basil

The most commonly used basil is the sweet or Genoa variety which is much favoured in Italian cooking. Thai or holy basil is used in Thai and South-East Asian dishes. To get the most out of basil leaves they should always be torn not chopped.

betel leaves

These are the aromatic, lacy-edged green leaves from the betel pepper. They can be found in Indian shops.

black sesame seeds

Mainly used in Asian cooking, black sesame seeds add colour, crunch and a distinct nuttiness to whatever dish they garnish. They can be found in most Asian grocery stores. Purchase the seeds regularly, as they can become rancid with age.

bocconcini

These are small balls of mozzarella, often sold sitting in their own whey. When fresh they are soft and springy to the touch and taste distinctly milky. They are available from most delicatessens.

brown miso

Brown miso (hatcho miso) is a fermented paste of soya beans, salt and either rice or barley. Miso is used extensively in Japanese cooking, in soups, dressings, stocks and as an ingredient in sauces and pickles. Brown miso has a richer flavour than white miso. It is available from Asian shops and health food stores.

butter puff pastry

This is puff pastry made with butter rather than vegetable fat, which gives it a much more buttery flavour than standard puff. If you can't find any, use ordinary puff pastry and brush it with melted butter to add flavour.

bulghur wheat

Popular in the Middle East, bulgur is the key ingredient in tabouli and pilaff. Steamed and baked to minimise cooking time, you can buy these wheat kernels either whole or cracked into fine, medium or coarse grains.

casareccia

These short lengths of rolled and twisted Italian pasta are traditionally served with a meat sauce.

capers

Capers are the green buds from a Mediterranean shrub, preserved in brine or salt. Salted capers have a firmer texture and are often smaller than those preserved in brine. Rinse away the brine or salt before using them. Capers are available from good delicatessens.

chocolate

Couverture is the best quality chocolate to use. This bittersweet chocolate contains the highest percentage of cocoa butter. Available from good delicatessens and food stores.

Chinese black beans

These salted black beans can be found either vacuum-packed or in tins in Asian food stores.

Chinese black vinegar

This rice vinegar is sharper than white rice varieties and is traditionally used in stir-fries, soups and dipping sauces. The Chinese province of Chekiang has the reputation for producing the best black vinegars.

Chinese five-spice power

This aromatic mix of ground spices is made up from black pepper, star anise, fennel seeds, cassia and cloves.

chipotle chillies

Chipotle chillies are available from delicatessens and specialty stores in tins where they are preserved in a smoky rich sauce or they can be bought as large smoked and dried chillies which need to be reconstituted in warm water prior to use.

ciabatta
Italian for "slipper", this loaf of bread is supposed to be in the shape of a shoe. Very light and with a porous texture, the Italians favour this loaf for sandwiches.

cinnamon
Commonly sold in powdered form, cinnamon can also be bought in long "quills" of bark approximately 1 metre long.

coconut cream
Slightly thicker than coconut milk, coconut cream is available in tins. If you can't get hold of it, use the thick cream off the top of a couple of tins of coconut milk instead. Pour the milk into a jug and leave it to settle — the cream will separate out at the top.

cream
Cream comes with differing fat contents. If it needs to be whipped it must have a fat content higher than 35 per cent. Single and light cream cannot be whipped.

cream of tartar
This fine white powder is the acidic ingredient in baking powder and is used to stablize egg whites.

crème fraîche
A naturally soured cream which is lighter than sour cream, it is available at gourmet food stores and some large supermarkets.

curry leaves
These are the smallish green aromatic leaves of a tree native to India and Sri Lanka. Curry leaves give a distinctive flavour to south Indian dishes. They are usually either fried and added to the dish or used as a garnish at the end.

daikon
Daikon, or mooli, is a large white radish. Its flavour varies from mild to quite spicy, depending on the season and variety. Daikon contains an enzyme that aids digestion. It can be freshly grated or slow-cooked in broths, and is available from most large supermarkets or Asian grocery stores. Select firm and shiny vegetables with unscarred skins.

dashi granules
These can be made into instant dashi stock simply by adding boiling water.

dried porcini mushrooms
Dried porcini (cep) mushrooms can be found either in small packets or sold loose from a jar in delicatessens.

enoki mushrooms
These pale, delicate mushrooms have a long thin stalk and tiny caps. They are very fragile and need only a minimal cooking time.

feta cheese
Feta is a white cheese made from sheep's milk or goat's milk. The fresh cheese is salted and cut into blocks before being matured in its own whey. It must be kept in the whey or in oil during storage or it will deteriorate quickly. Persian feta is particularly creamy in style. Feta is available from delicatessens and most supermarkets.

fish sauce
This is a highly flavoured, salty liquid made from fermented fish and widely used in South Asian cuisine to give a salty, savoury flavour. Buy a small bottle and keep it in the fridge.

French beans
This green bean is a very thin variety that is crisp and tender. Also known as string beans, they can also have yellow, purple or cream pods.

fresh horseradish
Fresh horseradish is a large white root with a knobbly brown skin. It is very pungent with a spicy, hot flavour.

galangal
Very popular in Thai cooking, galangal has a gingery flavour. This rhizome is from the same family as ginger.

gelatine leaves
Sheet gelatine is available in leaves of varying sizes. Be careful to check the manufacturer's instructions regarding liquid and gelantine sheet ratios. If leaves are unavailable, use gelatine powder instead, making sure it is well dissolved in the warm liquid.

goat's curd
This is a soft, fresh cheese made from goat's milk. It has a slightly acidic but mild and creamy flavour.

haloumi cheese
Haloumi is a semi-firm sheep's milk cheese. It has a rubbery texture which becomes soft and chewy when the cheese is grilled or fried. It is available from delicatessens and most large supermarkets.

haricot beans
Famous for their use in baked beans, there are several main types of haricot beans — cannellini and flageolets. In the United States and Europe, they are also known as white beans.

Indian lime pickle
Lime pickle is available from Indian grocery stores or large supermarkets. It is usually served as a side dish in Indian cooking.

jalapeno chillies
Small pickled jalapeno chillies are available in jars in the Mexican or gourmet section of specialty stores and large supermarkets. They add a sweet but fiery bite to many salsas and like most chillies should be used with a light hand or to personal taste.

Japanese eggplant
Much smaller and straighter in shape than the conventional eggplant or aubergine, the Japanese variety also has softer and slightly sweeter flesh.

kipfler potatoes
These small, elongated potatoes with yellow waxy flesh are ideal for boiling.

lamb's lettuce
This salad green is also known as corn salad or mâche. Its narrow, dark green leaves have a delicious nutty flavour.

lemon grass
These long fragrant stems are very popular in Thai cuisine. The tough outer layers should be stripped off first and it can then be used either finely chopped or whole in soups. Lemon grass can be stored for up to 2 weeks.

makrut leaves
Also known as the kaffir lime, the glossy leaves of this South-East Asian tree impart a wonderful citrusy aroma. Always try and use fresh, rather than dried leaves.

marsala
Perhaps Italy's most famous fortified wine, marsala is available in sweet and dry varieties. Often used in desserts such as zabaglione, it is a superb match with eggs, cream and almonds.

mascarpone cheese
This heavy, Italian-style set cream is used as a base in many sweet and savoury dishes. It is available from good delicatessens and supermarkets.

mesclun
Mesclun is a green salad mix originating in Provence, France. This salad often contains a selection of young, small leaves.

mint
Mint comes in many different varieties including peppermint, spearmint and applemint, but the common garden variety is wonderful in salads or as a garnish.

mirin
Mirin is a rice wine used in Japanese cooking. It adds sweetness to many sauces and dressings, and is used for marinating and glazing dishes like teriyaki. It is available from Asian grocery stores and most large supermarkets.

mizuna
These tender young salad leaves have a pleasant, peppery flavour

mozzarella
Fresh mozzarella can be found in most delicatessens and is easily identified by its smooth, white appearance and ball-like shape. It is not to be confused with mass-produced mozzarella, which is mostly used as a pizza topping. Mozzarella is usually sold packed in whey.

mustard seeds
Mustard seeds have a sharp, hot flavour that is tempered by cooking. Both brown and yellow are available, although brown mustard seeds are more common.

orecchiette
Orecchiette simply means 'little ears' in Italian and it is easy to see how these tiny discs of pasta earned their name.

orange flower water
This perfumed distillation of bitter-orange blossoms is mostly used as a flavouring in baked goods and drinks. It is available from delicatessens and large supermarkets.

oyster mushrooms
These beautifully shaped, delicately flavoured mushrooms are commonly greyish brown in colour but are also available in pink and yellow varieties.

oyster sauce
Made from oysters, brine and soy sauce, this thick brown sauce is a popular Asian seasoning.

palm sugar

Palm sugar is obtained from the sap of various palm trees and is sold in hard cakes or cylinders and in plastic jars. If it is very hard it will need to be grated. It can be found in Asian grocery stores or large supermarkets. Substitute dark brown sugar when palm sugar is unavailable.

pancetta

Pancetta is salted belly of pork. It is sold in good delicatessens, especially Italian ones, and some supermarkets. Pancetta is available either rolled and finely sliced or in large pieces ready to be diced or roughly cut. It adds a rich bacon flavour to dishes.

panettone

An aromatic northern Italian yeast bread made with raisins and candied peel, panettone is traditionally eaten at Christmas, when it is found in most Italian delicatessens and large supermarkets. Tiny ones are also available.

papaya

This large tropical fruit can be orange, red or yellow. This interesting fruit contains an enzyme which will stop gelatine from setting so avoid using it in any jellies. Sometimes called a pawpaw, they are really part of the custard apple family.

pesto

Available ready-made in most supermarkets, pesto is a puréed sauce traditionally made from basil, garlic, Parmesan cheese, pine nuts and olive oil.

pickled ginger

Japanese pickled ginger is available from most large supermarkets. The thin slivers of young ginger root are pickled in sweet vinegar and turn a distinctive salmon-pink colour in the process. (Bright pink ginger has been dyed.) The vinegar is an ideal additive to sauces where a sweet, gingery bite is called for.

pine mushrooms

Also known as matsutake, these Japanese mushrooms are brown in colour and thick and meaty in texture. They are best if cooked simply.

pink peppercorns

These are not true peppercorns but rather the aromatic dried red berries from the tree Schinus molle.

plain yoghurt

Where recipes call for plain yoghurt use a good, thick variety like Greek or Greek-style. If the yoghurt seems watery, drain it in a muslin-lined sieve for about 2 hours.

pomegranate molasses

This is a thick syrup made from the reduction of pomegranate juice. It has a bittersweet flavour, which adds a sour bite to many Middle Eastern dishes. It is available from Middle Eastern specialty stores. The closest substitute is sweetened tamarind.

preserved lemon

These are whole lemons preserved in salt or brine, which turns their rind soft and pliable. Just the rind is used — the pulp should be scraped out and thrown away. It is available from delicatessens.

prosciutto

Prosciutto is lightly salted, air-dried ham. It is most commonly bought in paper-thin slices, and is available from delicatessens and large supermarkets. Parma ham and San Daniele are both types of prosciutto.

puy lentils

Originally grown in the volcanic soils of the Puy region in France, these lentils are highly prized for their flavour and the fact that they hold their shape during cooking.

rice wine vinegar

Made from fermented rice, this vinegar comes in clear, red and black versions. Where just rice wine vinegar is called for, use the clear version.

ricotta cheese

Ricotta cheese can be bought cut from a wheel or in tubs. The wheel tends to be firmer in consistency and is better for baking. If you can only get ricotta in tubs, drain off any excess moisture by letting it sit for a couple of hours in a muslin-lined sieve.

risoni

Risoni are small rice-shaped pasta.

risotto rice

There are three well-known varieties of risotto rice that are widely available today: arborio, a large plump grain that makes a stickier risotto; vialone nano, a shorter grain that gives a loose consistency but keeps more of a bite in the middle; and carnaroli, similar in size to vialone nano, which makes a risotto with a firm consistency. All are interchangeable, although cooking times may vary by 5 minutes or so.

rose-water

The distilled essence of rose petals, rose-water is used to impart a perfumed flavour to pastries and sweet puddings. It is available from delicatessens and large supermarkets.

saffron threads

These are the orange-red stigmas of a type of crocus. Saffron is expensive and should be bought in small quantities. Use it sparingly as it has a very strong flavour.

sambal oelek

A hot paste made from pounded chillies, salt and vinegar, it is available from Asian grocery stores and most large supermarkets.

sesame oil

Sesame oil is available in two varieties. The darker, more pungent, type is made with roasted sesame seeds and comes from China, while a paler, non-roasted variety is Middle Eastern in origin.

shiitake mushrooms

These Asian mushrooms have white gills and a brown cap. Meaty in texture, they keep their shape very well when cooked. Dried shiitake are often sold as dried Chinese mushrooms.

Sichuan pepper

This is made from the dried red berries of the prickly ash tree, which is native to Sichuan in China. The flavour given off by the berries is spicy-hot and leaves a numbing aftertaste which can linger for some time. Dry-fry and crush the berries for the best flavour. Japanese sancho pepper is a close relative of Sichuan pepper and may be used instead.

smoked rainbow trout

Smoked rainbow trout is sold either as a whole fish or vacuum-packed as fillets. It can be hot-smoked or cold-smoked. Remember to remove any small bones before using it.

smoky paprika

Paprika is commonly sold as a dried, rich red powder made from a member of the chilli family. It comes in many grades from delicate through to sweet and finally hot. Smoky paprika from Spain adds a distinct rich and smoky flavour and is worth looking for if you enjoy introducing these flavours into your favourite dishes.

somen noodles

These thin, wheat-based Japanese noodles are commonly sold dried and in bundles. They are available from Japanese specialty stores, Asian supermarkets and health food stores.

star anise

This is a pretty, star-shaped dried fruit that contains small, oval, brown seeds. Star anise has a flavour similar to that of anise but is more liquorice-like. It is commonly used whole because of its decorative shape.

sumac

Sumac is a peppery, sour spice made from dried and ground sumac berries. The fruit of a shrub found in the northern hemisphere, it is typically used in Middle Eastern cookery. It is available from most large supermarkets and Middle Eastern specialty stores.

Swiss brown mushrooms

These mushrooms have a stronger flavour and texture than the common mushroom. Larger specimens are known as portobello mushrooms.

tahini

This is a creamy paste made from ground sesame seeds. It is available in jars from most supermarkets.

tamarind

Tamarind is the sour pulp of an Asian fruit. It is most commonly available compressed into cakes or refined as tamarind concentrate in jars. Tamarind concentrate is widely available; the pulp can be found in Asian food shops. To make tamarind water from compressed tamarind, put 100 g (3 1/2 oz) of tamarind into a bowl and cover with 500 ml (2 cups) of boiling water. Allow to steep for 1 hour, stirring occasionally to break up the fibres, then strain. Use the concentrate according to the package instructions.

tamari

A naturally brewed Japanese soy sauce made from fermented soya beans, rice, water and salt.

tofu

This white curd is made from soya beans and is a great source of protein. Bland in taste, it takes on the flavour of the other ingredients. Usually sold in blocks, there are several different types of tofu — soft (silken), firm, sheets and deep-fried.

tortillas

This thin, round, unleavened bread is used in Mexican cooking as a wrap. Tortillas are available prepackaged in the refrigerator section of most supermarkets.

truss tomatoes

Truss simply means tomatoes which can be brought on the vine.

turmeric

Often called poor man's saffron, never use the golden-coloured turmeric in place of the real thing. Turmeric is made from the root of a tropical plant related to ginger.

vanilla

The long slim black vanilla bean has a wonderful caramel aroma which synthetic vanillas can never capture. Good quality beans should be soft and not too dried. Store a vanilla pod in a jar of sugar and the flavour of the bean will quickly enfuse the sugar.

Vietnamese mint

Vietnamese mint is actually not really a true mint. Also known as hot mint or laksa mint, its spicy flavour is usually found paired with spring rolls and laksas.

vine leaves

The large, green leaves of the grapevine are available packed in tins, jars or plastic packs or in brine. They are used in Greek and Middle Eastern cookery to wrap foods for cooking. Vine leaves in brine should be rinsed before use to remove some of the salty flavour. Fresh, young vine leaves can be simmered in water for 10 minutes or until soft.

walnut oil

To preserve this oil's delicious nutty flavour, it is best to either keep it in the fridge or store it in a cool place out of direct sunlight for up to 3 months. This versatile oil is great used in salad dressings, sauces and baking.

water chesnuts

The edible tuber of a water plant, the water chestnut is white and crunchy and adds a delicate texture to many South-East Asian dishes. Fresh water chestnuts can be bought at Chinese food stores, but they are commonly available whole or sliced in tins.

white miso

White miso (actually a pale yellow colour) is the fermented paste of soya beans, salt and either rice or barley. Miso is used extensively in Japanese cooking, in soups, dressings, stocks and as an ingredient in sauces and pickles. White miso has a sweet, mellow taste and a relatively low salt content. It is available from Asian grocery stores and health food stores.

witlof

Also called Belgian endive or chicory, this salad leaf has a bitter flavour and crisp, crunchy texture when raw. You can find witlof in both pale yellow and purple varieties.

won ton wrappers

These paper-thin sheets of dough are available either fresh or frozen from Asian grocery stores. They may be wrapped around fillings and steamed, deep-fried or used in broths. The wrappers come shaped both as squares and circles and are available in various thicknesses.

young ginger

Without the woody texture of older ginger, younger ginger can come with a green stem attached and a softer, yellow skin. Its flavour is not as strong or hot as old ginger.

bibliography

Alexander, Stephanie. *The Cook's Companion*. Penguin Books, 1996.

David, Elizabeth. *Summer Cooking.* Penguin Books, 1955.

Grigson, Sophie and Black, William. *Fish*. Headline Book Publishing, 2000.

Jaffrey, Madhur. A Taste of India. Pavillion Books, 1985

Kennedy, Diana. Mexican Regional Cooking. Harper Perrenial, 1990

Roden, Claudia. A New Book of Middle Eastern Food, Penguin Books, 1986

Roden, Claudia. *Mediterranean Cookery*. BBC Books, 1987.

Sahni, Julie. Savouring Spices and Herbs, Morrow, 1996

Shaida, Margaret. The Legendary Cuisine of Persia, Penguin Books 1994

Solomon, Charmaine. *Encyclopedia of Asian Food.* New Holland Publishers, 2000.

Trang, Corinne. *Authentic Vietnamese Cooking*. Headline Book Publishing, 1999.

index